PIRATES
THEN AND NOW
Notorious Outlaws of the Sea

KATHY CAMPBELL &
MICHAEL FLEEMAN

CENTENNIAL BOOKS

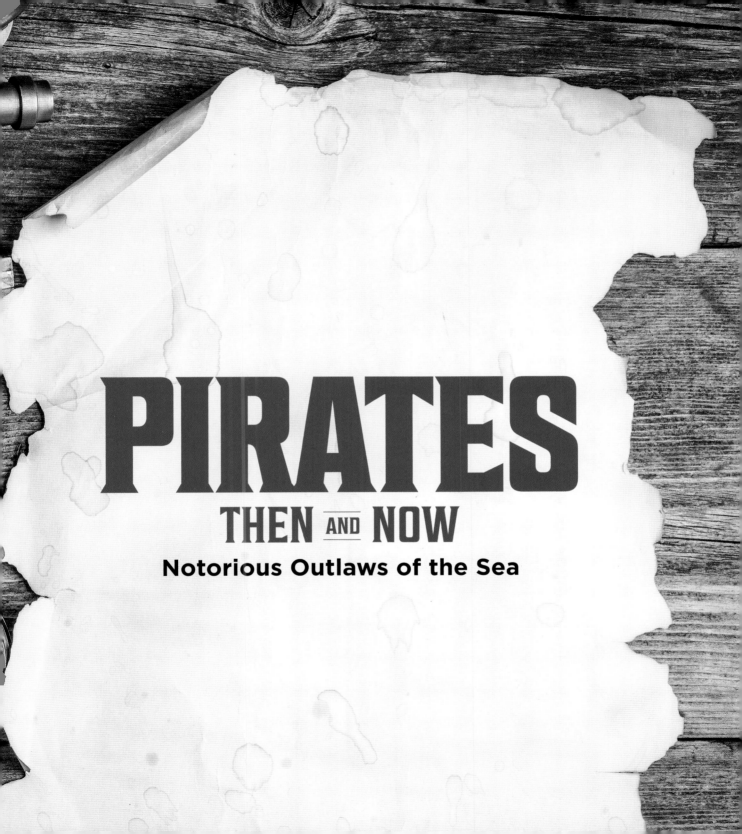

PIRATES

THEN AND NOW

Notorious Outlaws of the Sea

Contents

26

10

178

A Pirate's Life, Indeed!

Despite questionable morals and often barbaric behaviors, their fighting spirit and sense of adventure still hold appeal

In 1724, *A General History of the Pyrates* rolled off the London presses and made icons of Blackbeard, Henry Every, "Calico" Jack Rackham, Black Bart and the spirited female duo Anne Bonny and Mary Read. Nearly 300 years later, pirates still fascinate us. We flock to the *Pirates of the Caribbean* films, dress like pirates for Halloween, and talk like a pirate one day every September. We eat at pirate-themed restaurants. We can all even hum "A Pirate's Life for Me."

In these pages, unlock the secrets of pirates and piracy. Get to know the colorful cutthroats of history, like the dashing privateer Sir Francis Drake and William Dampier, the pirate with gourmet tastes who introduced the world to guacamole. Explore what life was really like on a pirate ship, from the practical reasons behind their lively fashion choices (some thought hoop earrings thwarted seasickness) to why they flew the Jolly Roger.

They were a gritty bunch, but surprisingly ahead of their time. Only pirates democratically elected their own captains—and sacked them when they didn't measure up. Discover why this curious subculture held progressive attitudes toward race, religion and even gender. For all their love of raping and whoring around, pirates would also fight alongside women and take orders from female leaders like the legendary Ching Shih, who commanded a mighty fleet of her own.

This strange and colorful cast of characters stirred the imaginations of storytellers like Robert Louis Stevenson and J.M. Barrie, whose notable creations—Long John Silver, Captain Hook—are the pirate prototypes who inspired swashbuckling stars Errol Flynn, Douglas Fairbanks, Maureen O'Hara and Johnny Depp. And the reason we believe pirates roll their R's and say things like "Shiver me timbers" is because of actor Robert Newton.

To be sure, the popularization of pirates has served to water down the more unsavory aspects of their existence—they were, after all, fundamentally thieves and could act quite savagely—and the line between reality and myth has not so much been blurred but obliterated. They can be anything we want them to be, to the point that we can reasonably picture pirates dancing like Gene Kelly and singing like Kevin Kline, sacking a city or haunting a ghost ship.

But no matter the buccaneer, real or fiction, their spirit of rebellion and thirst for freedom and adventure endures. Pirates were loud, brash, flamboyantly dressed, upending social norms and sticking it to the ruling classes. Like Captain Jack Sparrow, they were the original rock stars in many ways. Yet unlike real rockers, they have managed to age particularly well, and as we live through them vicariously and enthusiastically, their spirit remains felt today.

—*Michael Fleeman*

A few legendary treasure chests may still lie undiscovered on a deserted island or at the bottom of the sea.

CHAPTER 1

SCOURGE OF THE SEAS

*Hoist the Jolly Roger and seek out this treasure trove
of buccaneer basics that every cutthroat should know,
from pirates' at-sea menus to their cruelest punishments*

A Colorful and

A time line tracing the origins of pirates from ancient times to today

Sea Peoples defeated by Ramses III

Palace of Knossos, Crete

1300 B.C.

Mediterranean Marauders

The first recorded pirates, called the Lukkans, are based along the coast of modern Turkey and raid Cyprus in the 14th century B.C., according to Egyptian scribes. They ally themselves with the Hittite Empire and harass the Egyptians before joining other nomadic sailors in a group called the Sea Peoples. Carvings of a battle between the Sea Peoples and Ramses III's fleet off the Nile Delta depict what are believed to be the first pirate-like images in history.

1200 B.C.

Plundering Greece

Crete is a pirate haven for hundreds of years—Homer mentions Cretan pirates in the *Odyssey*—with outlaws raiding ships and settlements around the Aegean Sea. As Athens gains strength, the Cretans are replaced by northerners known as the Aetolians, while Greece's eastern shoreline teems with Illyrians and Dalmatians from what is now Croatia and Albania.

78 B.C.

Julius Caesar Is Kidnapped

Pirates become such a menace during Roman times that Cicero calls them *hostes humani generi*, or enemies of the human race. A young Julius Caesar is kidnapped by renegades and his noble family is forced to pay a ransom for his release. After Cilician pirates from what is now southeastern Turkey support Spartacus' slave revolt in 73 B.C. to 71 B.C., Rome's Pompey the Great leads an anti-piracy campaign— he's granted the powers of imperium —and wipes out the Cilicians, making Mediterranean waters safe for Roman ships for centuries.

798

Pillaging Vikings

While not technically pirates—since they raid on land, not sea, and become conquerors rather than just thieves— the Scandinavians in their swift oar-powered ships "go Viking." They rape, plunder and ravage England's coast for two centuries from A.D. 798 to A.D. 1066. and show a savage spirit that will always be associated with traditional pirates.

Julius Caesar

"Damn ye, you are a sneaking puppy, and so are all those who will submit to be governed by laws which rich men have made for their own security."

"BLACK SAM" BELLAMY

Bloody History

1216
Battling in the North Sea
As trade increases in the Atlantic and the English Channel, piracy flourishes, led by the Dover-based Eustace the Monk, who attacks French ships in the Channel around 1216 before turning on his homeland with an ill-fated French invasion of England, which punishes him with beheading. The North Sea becomes the domain of German pirate Klein Henszlein before his capture by merchants. He and 33 crewmen have their heads perched on stakes in public as a warning.

1343
A Vengeful Wife
Noblewoman Jeanne de Clisson avenges her husband's murder at the direction of King Philip VI by attacking French ships, earning the moniker "The Lioness of Brittany."

1531
The Rise of Red Beard
Muslim privateer Barbarossa captures Tunis from Spain and is named the grand admiral of the Ottoman Empire, though informally he is known as the King of the Sea.

Barbarossa

Vikings

Public executions

King Philip VI

1558

Elizabeth's Buccaneers

After Queen Elizabeth I takes the throne in 1558, privateering—led by famous captains like Francis Drake and Walter Raleigh—flourishes. These first-rate sailors find fame and fortune as legally sanctioned pirates attacking only ships from enemy Spain. Calling themselves buccaneers, these privateers scour the Spanish Main (Spanish-ruled coastal areas in the Caribbean)—which the country had claimed since Columbus' arrival in 1492—and capture the slow and cumbersome galleys laden with gold.

Grace O'Malley

1565

A Pirate Queen

As chieftain of the Irish O'Malley clan after her father's death, Grace O'Malley plunders English ships and defends her Irish homeland in brash defiance of Queen Elizabeth I, who eventually comes to respect her and grant her mercy in exchange for fighting for England.

1650

The Golden Age Begins

This is the year that many historians credit as the beginning of the Golden Age of Piracy. The end of the French Wars of Religion ushers in a period of colonial expansion for European countries, whose ships—heavy with gold, silver, silks, spices and other goods from their new colonies—fall prey to pirates. Based on the island of Tortuga, off Hispaniola, these buccaneers—who get their name from their habit of smoking meat on racks called *boucanes* in French—raid large, slow-moving Spanish galleons.

Pillaging of an American town in the 1600s

1651

Black Market Business

The Navigation Acts require English colonies, including America, to sell goods only to England and to import only English products, and conduct all trade using only English ships. This monopolizing means colonies have to sell products like tobacco at below-market prices and purchase luxuries like spices and silks at inflated prices—if the goods are available at all. This encourages a black market for privateers, who not only openly sell their goods in colonial ports but often are bankrolled by local businessmen and officials.

Elizabeth I

Walter Raleigh

Tortuga Island

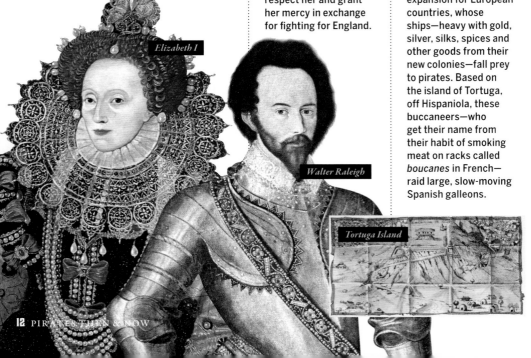

1655

The Real Pirates of the Caribbean

England captures Jamaica from Spain, granting letters of marque to Tortuga buccaneers to attack Spanish ships as privateers and providing protection and a market for them in the city of Port Royal, notorious for its taverns and brothels. The French governor of Tortuga also provides commissions to Englishmen from Port Royal, establishing the Caribbean as the world's haven for pirating.

1689

Looking Farther Afield

England's new peace with Spain and war with France denies English privateers the right to seize treasure-heavy Spanish merchant ships, leaving them with the less valuable—and much swifter—French ships. English and American privateers move on to the Red Sea to target Muslim ships of the Mughal Empire.

1694

Mutiny and a Bounty

The unhappy crew of the English privateer *Charles II*, a fighting ship with 46 cannons, stages a mutiny while the captain is drunk and picks the first officer, Englishman Henry Every, as captain, renaming the ship *Fancy* and launching the career of the infamous pirate. The next year, Every raids the Mughal ship *Fateh Mohammed*, hauling off booty worth $114 million today and ravaging their captives, with many of the raped women committing suicide by throwing themselves into the sea. Soon after, Every—who has a sizable bounty on his head in the first international manhunt—gives up his pirate career and disappears, possibly becoming one of the few pirates to live long enough to enjoy the spoils of his success.

1695

The Pirate Round

St. Mary's Island off the coast of Madagascar becomes a safe haven for Red Sea pirates who store their ships in secluded coves and distribute their loot among their crews. When privateer Thomas Tew returns with more than 100,000 pounds in gold and silver coin, along with silks, spices and elephant tusks from a Mughal vessel, piracy flourishes on the shipping route known as the Pirate Round that leads from the Western Atlantic, around the southern tip of Africa and on to the coast of Yemen and India. Tew is killed in 1695 while trying to capture another Mughal convoy.

1698

Kidd's Buried Treasure

"Captain" William Kidd seizes a fortune in gold, spices and silks from the Armenian ship the *Quedagh Merchant*, only to be betrayed by his benefactors and hanged as a pirate. Some of the booty he hid while on the run is later recovered, but treasure hunters have searched for generations for the rest of it, scouring locations in New York and New Jersey.

Captain Kidd

Sir Francis Drake

13

YOUNG FOLKS PAPER.
FOR OLD AND YOUNG BOYS AND GIRLS.

Treasure Island

Blackbeard

The Pirates of Penzance

Pauline Chase in Peter Pan

1724
Tall Tales
A General History of the Robberies and Murders of the Most Notorious Pyrates is published, providing the first and most enduring—if highly fictionalized—accounts of the deeds of iconic pirates, including Blackbeard, Bartholomew "Black Bart" Roberts and "Captain" William Kidd.

1801
The Widow Ching
A prostitute named Ching Shih begins her rise to become "The Terror of South China" when she marries a pirate fleet leader in 1801. After he dies, she weds his adopted son and commands a pirate empire of hundreds of junks and thousands of sailors.

1720
The End of the Golden Era
The Golden Age of Piracy comes to an end, the date placed roughly around the deaths of Blackbeard, Charles Vane and Bartholomew Roberts, and the captures of famous women pirates Anne Bonny and Mary Read.

1718
Blackbeard's Last Stand
Edward Teach, aka Blackbeard, blockades Charleston Harbor in his most audacious move as a pirate captain. Months later, Blackbeard is killed in a battle with colonial government forces, and his head is mounted on a pole over Chesapeake Bay as a warning to other pirates.

> *"It's better to swim in the sea below than to swing in the air and feed the crow, says jolly Ned Teach of Bristol."*
>
> BENJAMIN FRANKLIN, ON BLACKBEARD'S HANGING

1879
Lighthearted Laughs
Gilbert and Sullivan's comic opera *The Pirates of Penzance* opens in New York and London to rave reviews; it has charmed audiences worldwide for more than 140 years.

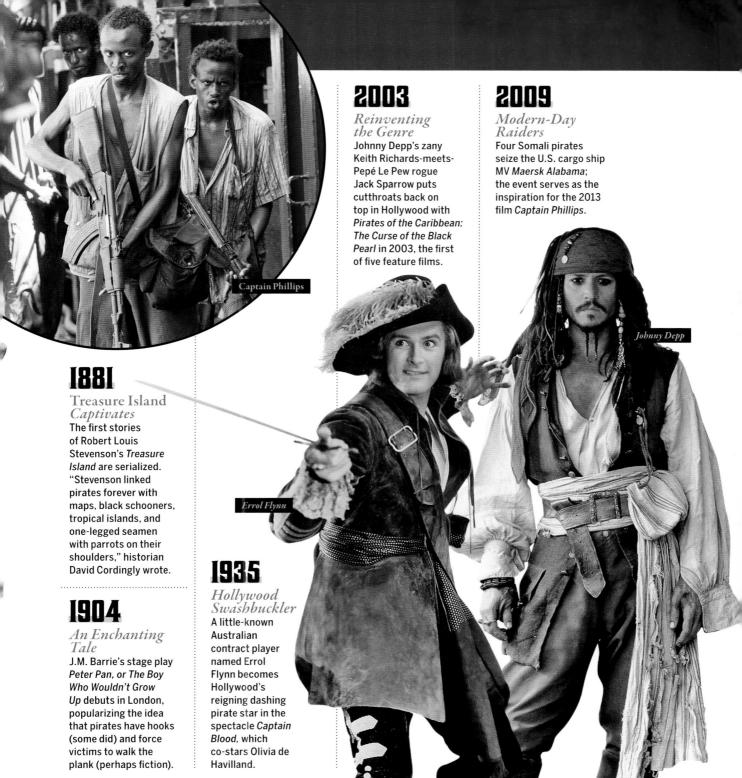

Captain Phillips

2003
Reinventing the Genre
Johnny Depp's zany Keith Richards-meets-Pepé Le Pew rogue Jack Sparrow puts cutthroats back on top in Hollywood with *Pirates of the Caribbean: The Curse of the Black Pearl* in 2003, the first of five feature films.

2009
Modern-Day Raiders
Four Somali pirates seize the U.S. cargo ship MV *Maersk Alabama*; the event serves as the inspiration for the 2013 film *Captain Phillips*.

Johnny Depp

1881
Treasure Island Captivates
The first stories of Robert Louis Stevenson's *Treasure Island* are serialized. "Stevenson linked pirates forever with maps, black schooners, tropical islands, and one-legged seamen with parrots on their shoulders," historian David Cordingly wrote.

1904
An Enchanting Tale
J.M. Barrie's stage play *Peter Pan, or The Boy Who Wouldn't Grow Up* debuts in London, popularizing the idea that pirates have hooks (some did) and force victims to walk the plank (perhaps fiction).

Errol Flynn

1935
Hollywood Swashbuckler
A little-known Australian contract player named Errol Flynn becomes Hollywood's reigning dashing pirate star in the spectacle *Captain Blood*, which co-stars Olivia de Havilland.

15

Why They Came Aboard

*Adventure, money and freedom lured many
a man, and boy, to a life as a sea wolf*

A young man who lacked the good fortune to be born into the elite classes in the 17th and 18th centuries could look forward to little more than a lifetime of toil in the fields or drudgery in a workshop—and that's if he didn't land in jail or the poorhouse.

That's why the sea had such a strong allure. A sailor's life aboard a merchant ship or navy vessel promised adventure, travel, danger and the possibility of upward social mobility. Then there was another option: piracy. The stakes were higher, but then, that was often the point.

At the start of the Golden Age of Piracy, in the mid-1600s, a man could experience all the piracy trappings—looting, pillaging, raping and killing—under the cover of a government license on a privateer ship.

As alliances shifted and privateering dried up, that meant going rogue. Around the world, the penalty for piracy was death by hanging, and the average pirate's career lasted only a few years. Yet many felt it was a risk worth taking.

The promise of wealth proved the most powerful motivation. A merchant or military seaman made a pittance, and even in the navy—which allowed for, and even encouraged, the taking of prizes—the captain and officers took such large shares it left little for the seamen.

Not so on pirate ships, which operated under much more democratic principles and distributed plunder more equitably, even if it all usually ended up in brothels and taverns. The captain was elected, and could be ousted by vote; this was a welcome accountability for former merchant and navy sailors who had endured tyrannical captains.

Freedom and fairness for regular men—alien concepts before the American and French revolutions—were rules to live by on pirate ships long before they were on land, and that sense of liberty extended to former slaves, either freed or escaped. Many crews were 30 to 50 percent Black, including Black officers.

More than anything, piracy offered adventure and rebellion. Even men who were forced into piracy after their ships were raided embraced the life. Nowhere else could restless men openly indulge in drinking, gambling, stealing and women, all the while getting revenge on the country, religion, family, monarch or captain who had never cared for them. For many, even if it all ended with a musket ball—or a noose around the neck—it was worth it. ⚓

> *"Life at sea was hard and dangerous, and interspersed with life-threatening storms or battles."*
>
> DAVID MOORE,
> NORTH CAROLINA
> MARITIME MUSEUM

"Yes, I do heartily repent," one pirate said as he headed to the gallows. "I repent I had not done more mischief."

THE YOUNGEST ROGUE

While teenage pirates were common in the 18th century, John King has the honor of being the youngest known pirate on record. The boy, aged between 8 and 11, was traveling with his parents on the Antiguan sloop the *Bonetta* when it was attacked by Samuel "Black Sam" Bellamy in November 1716. When the pirates held the ship for 15 days, King demanded to join the crew, declaring "he would kill himself if he was restrained," and even threatening his mother, according to the *Bonetta*'s commander, Abijah Savage. After initially refusing, Bellamy let him join the ship's crew. His time as a pirate was limited—five months later, Bellamy's ship, the *Whydah Gally*, was wrecked in a storm off Cape Cod, Massachusetts, killing Bellamy, King and all but two members of the 145-man crew. In 1984, the wreck of the *Whydah* was discovered. More than 100,000 artifacts were recovered over 20 years, including a small shoe, a silk stocking and a femur bone— all believed to belong to King, who was the only boy aboard. The remains are on display at the Whydah Pirate Museum in West Yarmouth, Massachusetts.

The Perils of Piracy

Pop culture buccaneers make it look fun—but in reality, it was a short, dangerous existence

During battles, hammocks would be rolled and stowed under railings as a barricade against musket fire.

A pirate's life may have been exhilarating and thrilling at times, but his day-to-day existence wasn't particularly romantic or glamorous.

"Life at sea was hard and dangerous, and was interspersed with life-threatening storms or battles," notes David Moore, curator of nautical archaeology at the North Carolina Maritime Museum. "There was no air-conditioning, ice for cocktails or clean sheets aboard the typical pirate ship."

WHERE THEY SLEPT

A pirate's day began with swaying. Like all mariners of the time, they slept in canvas hammocks because they swayed in sync with the movement of the ship for a more peaceful slumber. Dozens of hammocks were stretched out in a large sleeping area, while on some ships the men slept on the decks. Only captains and some higher-ranking pirates got their own staterooms.

With no dentists on board, as teeth rotted the easiest solution was to pull them out.

we use today weren't invented until 1938. If any care was taken of teeth at all, it was with a chew stick commonly used from ancient times through the 18th century. This lack of dental hygiene—combined with the ravages of scurvy, which was caused by a lack of vitamin C and rotted teeth down to the roots—caused bleeding gums and terrible breath.

WHAT THEY WORE

Pirates didn't have to dress for work because they slept in their clothes. The typical pirate look was eclectic; their wardrobe was cobbled together from what they once wore as a merchant or navy seaman, plus whatever they stole. That pirate getup of Halloween costumes—the tricorne (hat) with feather, jacket, breeches, hose and buckled shoes—was worn by pirate captains to flaunt their success and to ridicule the elite. For regular pirates, comfortable cotton muslin clothes were worn for work.

While some did wear the puffy shirt lampooned on *Seinfeld*, most pirates preferred tight shirts with open collars that wouldn't get snagged on rigging and gear. Garments would go long periods without washing and would show the wear and tear—rips, tears and mends—of their arduous labor. As for their pants, only pirate captains sported fancy breeches. Regular pirates wore loose-fitting canvas trousers. A scarf wrapped around the head kept the sweat out of the eyes and protected the neck from sunburn. A pirate's cloth sash around his waist also absorbed

DID THEY BATHE?

The close quarters, combined with the fact that pirates slept in their clothes and rarely took a bath, made for a smelly existence. Fresh water was precious, and was used for drinking, not washing. A plunge in the ocean was usually out of the question because most pirates, like other sailors of the era, didn't know how to swim, and there was always the risk that there were sharks in the water. Those who could swim would find the salt in seawater left them itchy. On the rare occasions they did bathe, the men would lather up with soap made from whale blubber.

GOING POTTY

There were no toilets on board. The "head" amounted to holes cut into planks over the open water, usually at the bow, or head, of the ship. In rough weather, pirates would avail themselves of a bucket and toss the waste overboard.

TOOTHBRUSHES DIDN'T EXIST

The reputation of pirates as having a mouth full of bad teeth is rooted in fact. Toothbrushes that

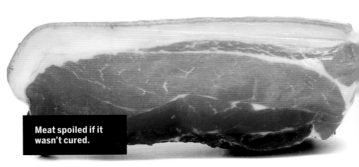

Meat spoiled if it wasn't cured.

sweat, and over that a big leather belt helped prevent back strain and hernias caused by heavy lifting. Most pirates worked sans shoes for better traction on wet decks and climbing rigging. (For more on common pirate garb for both the captain and the crew, see page 26.)

HOW THEY CHOWED DOWN

Food was served to a group, or "mess," of men in buckets they would share, and if they were lucky, they had square-shaped plates of wood or pewter for their "square meals." Pirates had notoriously bad table manners. One contemporary observer said pirate captain Edward Low's men ate "like a kennel of hounds...snatching and catching the victuals from one another." While on "Black Sam" Bellamy's ship, the *Whydah*, the crew used knives, forks and spoons to eat off pewter plates, a lot of pirates were only equipped with knives that they used to spear their food, using a hardtack biscuit as a scoop.

WHEN THE FOOD RAN OUT

The longer pirates stayed away from shore, the more hunger became a factor. Pirate captains were known to kidnap victims and ransom them for heads of cattle; during raids they seized not only gold, silver and jewels, but also food, water, beer and rum.

IN THEIR DOWNTIME

While their duties kept them busy at times, endless days spent at sea could become tedious if the sailors didn't have some forms of entertainment to distract from the drudgery. Some ships had musicians on board, and captains encouraged their men to sing sea shanties to keep up the morale. Card games, usually for money, were also common. Poker hadn't been invented yet, but the Irish played a game called Maw, while Spaniards and others faced off with early versions of Blackjack called One & Thirty and Bone Ace. Cribbage was also popular, as were games that used dice. ⚓

When pirates weren't plundering, they were assigned tasks related to the maintenance of the ship.

"They had a mail system— ships ferrying letters back and forth—that enabled them to communicate with relatives."

AUTHOR DAPHNE PALMER GEANACOPOULOS

Meet the

It wasn't all drinking, singing and gambling—pirate ships needed skilled crews who were assigned specific duties

A naval background was helpful to have.

CAPTAIN

In the biggest deviation from the navy and merchant marines, pirate crews elected their own captains and could replace them at will. The captains tended to be more accessible and lenient, responsive to their crews' needs and concerns. So drinking and gambling were tolerated, and the crew could wander into the captain's quarters at will—all of which would be unthinkable outside of a pirate ship. Pirate captains also couldn't inflict the same sort of severe and often arbitrary punishments carried out by their merchant and naval counterparts, who were notorious for lashing to the masts, flogging and maiming sailors for even minor transgressions. Instead, pirate captains had to follow the same rules as everybody

GUNNERS As the leaders of the crews of four or five men firing the cannons, the gunners—the most senior was called a master gunner, an elected position—usually were trained in the navy but had to alter their skills when they took up piracy. Pirates wanted to disable, not destroy, targeted ships to keep them as prizes, so gunners had to aim with particular precision. It was also one of the most dangerous jobs, because cannons frequently misfired, sometimes with deadly consequences. Outside of battle, gunners cleaned and repaired the weapons and managed the stock of ammunition and gunpowder.

Crew

else—except during battle, the only time pirate captains exercised total authority.

QUARTERMASTER

The second-in-charge, the quartermaster—also selected by the crew—assisted the captain and oversaw day-to-day operations, keeping track of food, water and supplies. He also served as advocate for the sailors. It was up to the quartermaster to mete out discipline—he could even punish the captain if necessary. The quartermaster led the boarding operations of targeted ships and was in charge of dividing the plunder among the crew. He would also become the captain of a captured ship.

BOATSWAIN

The equivalent of a junior officer, the boatswain, or bosun, reported to the quartermaster and captain and—depending on the size of the ship—managed the supplies and led shore parties to get water, food and other essentials. The best friend of the common sailor, he also supervised day-to-day duties, like the swabbing of the deck, the setting of sails and the dropping of the anchor.

CARPENTER

Usually reporting to the boatswain, the carpenter's job was to keep the ship—nearly all of which was made of wood—seaworthy.

A pirate captain ruled at the mercy of his crew.

MUSICIANS Among the most popular members of the crew, musicians entertained the men during the long, boring stretches between raids and provided motivation during battle. Since few sailors knew how to play instruments, trained musicians were usually abducted from other ships, and even land, and pressed into piracy. To keep them happy, they were often given larger shares of the stolen swag and could have the Sabbath off.

They were tasked with repairing the damage that was caused by battles and also supervised the periodic beaching of ships in order to make repairs and to scrape the hulls clean. Since most pirate ships lacked a trained surgeon, carpenters were also called upon to amputate mangled and gangrenous limbs, using the very same tools they employed to work on wood.

SAILING MASTER

Holding one of the most difficult jobs on any ship, the sailing master, or navigator, monitored the ship's location and charted the journey as well as possible in an era of inaccurate or nonexistent maps and primitive navigation tools. The sailing master relied heavily on the position of the sun and the stars; he would also frequently pilot the ship. Because this was a position requiring both skill and experience, a sailing master would be among the first people targeted by opposing crew members during boarding raids—even before treasure—and captured navigators were forced to serve on pirate ships.

COOPERS

These skilled builders of wooden barrels were also the most prized members of pirate ship crews, since water and food were usually stored in these important drums. They built new casks and maintained the old ones.

MATES

The apprentices to the quartermaster, gunner, carpenter and boatswain, the mates ensured that ropes, tackle, anchor and cables were in proper condition and they oversaw the mooring of the ship when it was in port. Ships had multiple mates, thus the positions of first, second and third mates.

CABIN BOYS AND POWDER MONKEYS

These young boys of 12 or 13, who either were kidnapped or ran away, worked as servants (cabin boys); others were powder monkeys who ran gunpowder from lower decks to the cannons during battles. ⚓

"People have this romantic notion of piracy, but it was not a cushy life."

KIMBERLY KENYON, FIELD DIRECTOR
FOR EXCAVATION OF BLACKBEARD'S SHIP,
QUEEN ANNE'S REVENGE

ABLE-BODIED SAILORS The majority of the crew, these were the common sailors who carried out the tasks on the ship under the direction of the boatswain and mates. Though usually illiterate and semiskilled, they still needed to know a wide variety of nautical skills: how to read the weather, conduct simple navigation readings, work the rigging and steer the ship. Sailors who mopped the deck using a swab (mop) were known as swabbies.

Dressed to Kill in Silk and Gold

Did buccaneers adorn themselves like Johnny Depp's Jack Sparrow?

Feathered hat, belted waistcoat and sword in hand, pirate captains were ready to lead their crews to battle.

Pirates definitely had their own form of fashion, but it wasn't necessarily the prototypical gilded waistcoat, ruffled shirt, breeches, hose and oversized hat (topped with a large plume) that *Peter Pan*'s Captain Hook paraded around deck in and that we think of as a pirate costume for Halloween. For most of the crew, clothing was a far more practical affair,

worn largely to accommodate their grueling work and the combined ravages of the sun, wind and salt water.

WHAT THE CREW WORE

Shirt | While 17th- and 18th-century shirts did tend to be puffier than today's versions, the pirate crews usually wore tight shirts with open collars to keep the cloth—which could be linen, cotton, wool or silk—from getting snagged on rigging and gear. Often stained, ripped and patched together, the shirts would always be tucked in for a reason unique to pirates: They didn't wear underwear and instead used the shirttails.

Pants | While many pirate captains showed off elaborate breeches, regular pirates favored loose-fitting canvas trousers for comfort and ease of movement while working.

Bandannas | A scarf wrapped around the head kept the sweat out of their eyes and kept the sun off the backs of their necks.

Belt and Sash | Wide leather belts protected pirates from back strain and hernias while lifting bulky cargo or hoisting ropes. A "pirate's sash" of cloth was wrapped around the waist under the belt to absorb sweat.

Shoes | While they were at sea, most pirates went barefoot, which helped them to get a better grip on the deck and while scampering up the ship's ropes and rigging.

"He liked expensive clothes, especially black coats. His favorite weapons were four dueling pistols that he always carried in the sash."

CAPTAIN SAMUEL BELLAMY,
DESCRIBED BY THEWAYOFTHEPIRATES.COM

Trousers varied in length from just below the knee to above the ankles.

Brass buckles
and shoes with
squared toes
have been found
on several
shipwrecks.

CAPTAINS WERE FANCIER DRESSERS

To show authority, and to just show off, pirate captains adopted the dress of merchant and naval officers as well as of gentlemen in a mash-up that was deliberately ridiculous, garish—and mostly stolen. The bright colors and ruffled flourishes—the hats, feathers and silks, the jewelry and weaponry— all became the branding statements of captains, making them walking billboards to their crews of the promise of more riches while also thumbing their noses at the upper-crust society members against whom they were rebelling—and robbing.

Tricorne | Popular during the 1600s and 1700s, the tricorne, also called a cocked hat, was popular with pirate captains, who often decorated their headwear with exotic bird feathers as symbols of the fabulous places they had gone.

Coat, Waistcoat, Breeches | The three-quarter-length coat, popular among gentlemen on land, was adopted by pirate captains. They were accentuated with bright-red velvet waistcoats (a sleeveless forerunner to a men's suit vest) and matching crimson breeches, trousers that ended just below the knee. Captains wore stockings made of silk, one of the most expensive commodities of the day and valued as much as gold and silver. Most, if not all, of these articles would likely have been stolen from naval officers' cabins during raids.

Jewelry | Gold chains, pendants, rings and earrings inlaid with jewels were worn by many captains to remind crew and foes alike of the pirates' successes as thieves—and to send a not-so-subtle warning to targeted ships of what they were about to lose.

Sash | A sash of leather and satin, decorated with gems, would be worn diagonally across the chest, then wrapped around the waist. From the sash captains would hang guns, knives and a cutlass.

Shoes and Buckles | For special occasions, captains would wear leather shoes with expensive buckles that were removable. But most of the time they would simply parade around in well-oiled, knee-high, heeled cavalier boots. ⚓

"*[They would drill a hole in a coin and] wear it on their wrist, or around their neck, so that no one could steal [it].*"

PIRATE HISTORIAN GAIL SELINGER

Long John Silver claimed his parrot was 200 years old and said "only the devil himself" had "seen more wickedness."

WERE PARROTS A PIRATE'S BEST FRIEND?

Long John Silver, the lead character in Robert Louis Stevenson's 1881 classic *Treasure Island*, clomped around with a missing leg and a parrot on his shoulder. As it turns out, the fictional character had a basis in reality—the birds were often found on pirate ships. While cats were prized for their ability to catch rats and mice in the holds of the ship, and monkeys were sometimes taken from islands as pets,

parrots were easier to have on board. They lived off nuts, fruit and seeds; could be taught tricks and to say colorful words and phrases to relieve boredom on long voyages; and were in no danger of falling overboard or drowning. When a ship was under attack, parrots could escape by flying into the rigging, while back in port they could be sold for a healthy profit to wealthy families who coveted the exotic creatures as pets.

What They Really Ate and Drank

There's a reason we don't have eat-like-a-pirate day

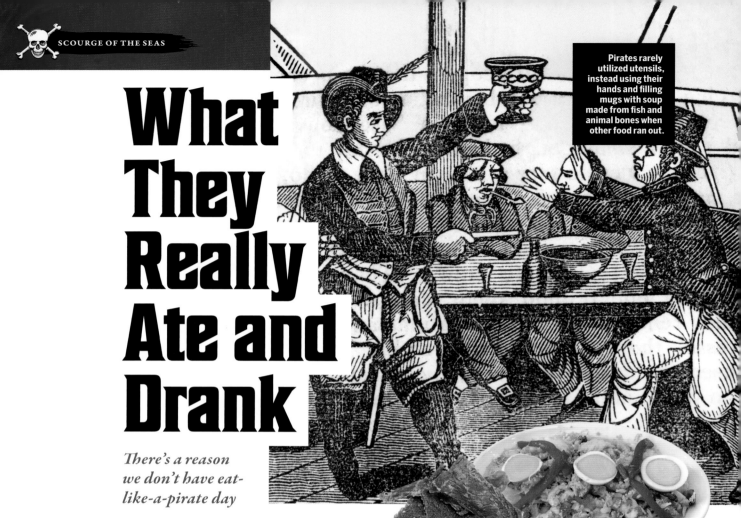

Pirates rarely utilized utensils, instead using their hands and filling mugs with soup made from fish and animal bones when other food ran out.

Salted beef

Salmagundi

On long voyages with no refrigeration, pirates ate poorly. They survived on unappetizing, unhealthy and meager rations of moldy bread, maggot-infested biscuits and salted beef. Perishable foods like fruit, vegetables, cheese, eggs, fresh beef and chicken ran out quickly—and the water on board was so bad that pirates chose to wash down their unappealing meals with beer and rum. This diet mirrored that of British merchant and navy sailors of the era, although the pirate's outlaw lifestyle meant they spent more time hiding out at sea with the constant specter of starvation.

THE PIRATE MENU

Hardtack | This staple for sailors around the world for generations was made of flour, salt and water, baked into a rock-hard biscuit. Because it was so dry, it was largely resistant to bacterial spoilage, but was often infested with weevils, which pirates simply flicked away before eating.

Salted Beef and Pork | Live cows, pigs and chickens provided fresh meat (plus milk and eggs) early in a cruise. Sea tortoises were also highly sought-after. But once all that was gone, sailors had to eat beef and pork that had been preserved with salt or air-dried into jerky-like strips that so closely resembled leather, sailors carved it into buttons or used it to patch holes in the ship.

Salmagundi | About the only pirate food anybody would eat today, this was a mishmash of wine-marinated roasted beef, ham, fish, sometimes pigeon or turtle, thrown into a stew with cabbage, dried beans, grapes, maybe anchovies and hard-boiled eggs, and served in a pile. To mask rancid meat, the dish was heavily seasoned with chili peppers, garlic, salt and pepper.

Rum | Along with up to a gallon of beer a day, pirates drank copious amounts of this potent drink made from fermented molasses. Alcoholic drinks lasted longer than water—and pirates lived under considerably looser rules. To maintain some sobriety, rum was usually mixed with water. When cinnamon or other flavorings were added to the mix, it was called grog (see recipe, right).

Booty | Since they often couldn't trade in port, pirates had to steal what they needed. During raids on ships or shore settlements, they went after food, water, beer and rum along with gold and silver. The longer they remained at sea, the more desperate they became, and hunger would drive them to eating their satchels and other leather items. One ship's crew even resorted to cannibalism. ⚓

HOW BUCCANEERS GOT THEIR NAME— FROM BARBECUE

The term "buccaneer" can be traced to the people of modern-day Haiti, who smoked meat over wooden racks that the French called *boucanes*. Their *viande boucanée*, or beef jerky, was sold to the pirates who attacked Spanish ships and settlements in the Caribbean, and eventually became known as buccaneers. Spaniards called the same method of cooking meat over a fire "barbacoa," which later became known as barbecue.

SIP LIKE A 1700s SAILOR

The recipe for the popular pirate potable grog is traced back to British Navy Vice Admiral Edward Vernon, known as "Old Grog" for wearing a coat of heavy cloth called grogram. Vernon's 1740 order to captains declared that his men's "pernicious custom" of drinking rum straight "cannot be better remedied than by ordering their half pint of rum to be daily mixed with a quart of water." To make the drink "more palatable," he ordered that they add sugar and lime juice.

Here's the vintage recipe for traditional "four water grog," with four parts water to one part rum.

- 16 ounces lime juice
- 1 pound brown sugar
- 1 pint dark rum
- ½ gallon water
- 6 sprigs mint

Mix the lime juice with the brown sugar, add to the blend of rum and water, toss in the mint, and you're ready to pillage.

Rum in barrels

Hardtack

Cruel and Very Unusual Punishments

To cross a fellow marauder meant starvation, drowning or a demented dance

A condemned man walks the plank in an 1887 illustration by Howard Pyle, whose images of pirate life influenced how we see the marauders today.

O ne of the advantages of being a pirate was that they could pretty much do whatever they wanted. A Pirate Code of Conduct, which varied from ship to ship, spelled out simple rules of safety and decorum, such as when and where to have open candles and when and where it was permissible to gamble or get drunk. Punishment was decided by the majority of the crew, who tended to opt for little or no punishment at all.

But even pirates had their limits. The most serious offenses were deserting a ship and failing to engage in battle. These would be met with the most severe punishment: marooning. The wrongdoer would be left on a remote island or sand spit without food or water. With no chance of being rescued, they would suffer a horrible death from thirst, starvation and the elements. If the other

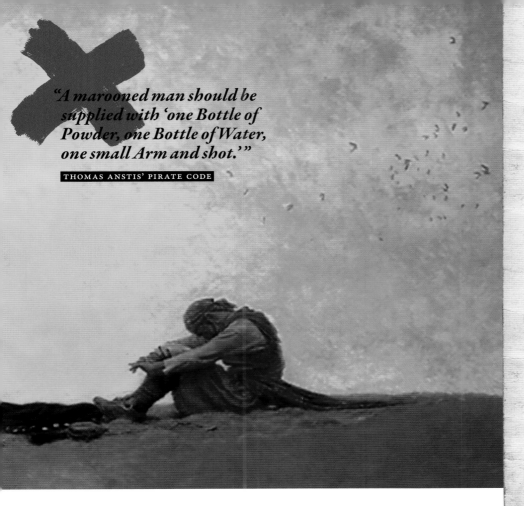

> "*A marooned man should be supplied with 'one Bottle of Powder, one Bottle of Water, one small Arm and shot.'*"
>
> **THOMAS ANSTIS' PIRATE CODE**

THE WORST TORTURE OF ALL

On land, a man sentenced to be drawn, hung and quartered was first tied to a wooden frame that was dragged by a horse to the gallows. The prisoner was then hanged until just shy of death. Next, his organs were drawn, or ripped out, before his ravaged body was slapped on a table and eviscerated some more before finally, his head was lopped off and the rest of his body was chopped into four parts. This was considered an acceptable form of punishment until the early 19th century, and it all started with a pirate: The first man subjected to this heinous torture was William Maurice of England, who was convicted of piracy in 1241. History says the punishment was specifically designed for him.

pirates were feeling charitable, they'd leave the wrongdoer with a loaded pistol to commit suicide.

Other forms of punishment included one well-known to all mariners of the day—flogging with a cat o' nine tails, which was a rope with nine strands that would be knotted or affixed with musket balls or fishhooks. Pirates could also be keelhauled—suspended by ropes from the yardarm with lead weights attached to their legs, after which they'd be tossed into the sea, where they'd scrape against the sharp barnacles of the keel.

They could also be tethered to the mast by a short rope and forced to "dance" while being poked with swords in a cruel game known as "sweating." Or they might simply be clapped in irons and dunked in the ocean a few times from a rope. Some were even sold into slavery.

If the authorities ever caught them, they faced only one punishment—hanging—as piracy was a capital offense the world over.

As for walking the plank, it had been known to happen, though not with the frequency or ceremony as seen in movies. The image of a blindfolded prisoner forced out at sword-point over the teeming seas appears for the first time in print in the 1724 book *A General History of the Robberies and Murders of the Most Notorious Pyrates* (though it's a ladder, not a plank) and became popular with fiction writers like Robert Louis Stevenson, author of *Treasure Island*, in the 1800s. Instead, pirates had a more expeditious form of this punishment: They simply tossed the person overboard. ⚓

Maps Were More Precious Than Jewels

These documents didn't point to treasure, but other valuables—
the location of new lands and sea lanes

"They were going to throw it overboard but by good luck I saved it," Sharp wrote in his journal of the map he copied and gave to King Charles II of England (pictured). "The Spaniards cried when I got the book."

When Captain Bartholomew Sharp returned to England in 1682 after an epic voyage to the New World, a tsunami of trouble awaited him.

During his travels, Sharp had engaged in widespread piracy, seizing the Spanish ship *Trinity* and proceeding to use it to pillage the entire Pacific Coast—waters that Spain had claimed.

The enraged Spanish ambassador demanded that England's King Charles II place Sharp's neck in a noose. But the wily captain had an insurance policy. Along with copious amounts of gold and silver, Sharp was able to present to the king the most valuable booty of all: a copy of a collection of nautical maps stolen from another ship. His hope was that this highly prized gift would save his life.

In those days, maps of the remote corners of the world were more prized than any treasure. Nations zealously guarded their own maps and went to great lengths to obtain charts from allies and enemies alike to help them navigate the unknown waters and distant lands.

In 1681, Sharp and his men sailed across the Atlantic and through the Caribbean Sea to Central America, where they made the arduous journey through the Isthmus of Panama to the Pacific. They grabbed the *Trinity* and raided dozens of other ships, including the Spanish vessel the *El Santo Rosario*. The pirates killed the captain and rummaged through the ship's haul, which at first

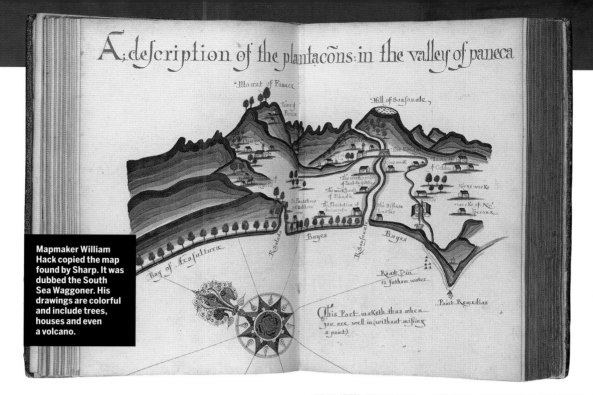

A description of the plantacõns in the valley of paneca

Mapmaker William Hack copied the map found by Sharp. It was dubbed the South Sea Waggoner. His drawings are colorful and include trees, houses and even a volcano.

appeared to be modest, mostly consisting of fruit and brandy. They tossed a bunch of silver metal overboard thinking it was tin, only to discover later, to their regret, it was a fortune in unrefined silver.

But Sharp's pirates did spot what one crewman described in his journal as "a great Book full of Sea Charts and Maps, containing a very accurate and exact description of all the Ports, Soundings, Creeks, Rivers, Capes and Coasts belonging to the South Sea, and all the Navigations usually performed by the Spaniards in that Ocean."

The Pacific Ocean was known then as the "South Sea," since it was south of the isthmus. Having been controlled by Spain for more than a century, the Spanish atlas, or *derrotero*, was so valuable that the *Rosario*'s pilot had tried to toss it overboard but had it wrenched from his hands.

Sharp made a colorful copy of the atlas, and, upon returning to England, gave it to King Charles II, who spared his life and made him a captain in the Royal Navy. The appointment proved short-lived as Sharp quickly returned to piracy. He died in prison in St. Thomas in the Danish West Indies in October 1702 at about age 52. ⚓

William Thompson

THE TREASURE OF LIMA

It's believed to be the greatest stash of pirate loot never found, an estimated $200 million in booty hidden by British Captain William Thompson. The treasure, believed to include a solid-gold, life-size, gem-encrusted statue of the Virgin Mary, had been entrusted to Thompson by Spanish authorities when they came under siege by revolutionaries in Lima, Peru, in 1820. Thompson double-crossed the Spanish, killing the guards and taking off on their ship *Mary Dear*. When Spanish forces tracked them down, the treasure was gone. Everyone on board was killed except Thompson and his first mate, who promised to reveal the location of the treasure in exchange for their lives. Instead, they escaped into the jungles of Cocos Island off Costa Rica. The men were never found—and neither was the Treasure of Lima. Treasure hunters have been looking for it ever since on the island, which inspired *Jurassic Park*'s Isla Nublar.

X Marks the Spot

The search for buried treasure continues

For all the stories of pirates squirreling away their gold and jewels on desert islands, the reality was that these rogues splurged so much on rum, women and gambling that they usually never had anything left to bury—although a few legendary booty stashes remain tantalizingly undiscovered.

BLACKBEARD'S BOOTY

Shortly before he was killed, Blackbeard may have purposely run his flagship, *Queen Anne's Revenge*, aground off North Carolina in 1718 so that he could run away and stash his fleet's booty to keep for himself. When salvage hunters found the shipwreck on the bottom of the ocean, none of the loot was there. Some speculate Blackbeard may have deposited the riches in a secret passage beneath the Bath Creek, North Carolina, estate of the state's colonial governor, Charles Eden, who had given Blackbeard a pardon—possibly in exchange for a cut.

CAPTAIN KIDD'S LOOT

After "Captain" William Kidd ran his leaky ship *Adventure Galley* aground in Madagascar in 1698, his crew deserted him for another pirate captain and Kidd was arrested and hanged. But what became of his riches? In 2015, divers found a 121-pound silver bar near the *Adventure Galley* wreck, raising hopes that more may one day be found underwater or on land. One possible burying spot is a place called Kidd's Ledge on Gardiners Island, off Long Island, New York, where he may have stopped before Madagascar.

Shortly after Kidd's capture, a cache of 200 bars of silver was found on Gardiners Island, along with a silver box inlaid with diamonds, a diamond ring and a casket containing 67 rubies, but the hoard uncovered is believed to be only a fraction of Kidd's real fortune. Before his death, Kidd proposed to the Earl of Bellomont that he could sail to St. Thomas Island and Curaçao in the Caribbean as the earl's prisoner to bring back a treasure worth £50,000 to £60,000 (approximately $64,000 to $77,000). He was turned down.

THOMAS TEW'S EMPTY CHEST

The privateer-turned-pirate Thomas Tew left behind an ornate 150-pound iron treasure chest painted with birds, flowers and angels in Newport, Rhode Island, in 1695, perhaps brought back aboard the *Amity* after raiding a Mughal ship of millions of dollars in treasure in the Indian Ocean. Alas, the chest was empty, although it was sold at auction in December 2000 for $63,450 to a former pro sports executive, who put it on display in his St. Augustine Pirate & Treasure Museum in Florida. ⚓

Ahead of Their Time

Buccaneers were surprisingly progressive when it came to many issues, including homosexuality and politics

Anne Bonny

Mary Read

Pirates may have looked like a rough-and-tumble lot, but they did adopt some practices that wouldn't take root more widely for centuries, such as tolerant attitudes toward homosexuality, race, religion and, to a limited degree, gender, along with cutting-edge ideas about health care and democracy.

GAY MARRIAGE

Well, almost. So-called "situational homosexuality" during long voyages was probably no more or less prevalent on pirate ships than any vessel—though it's impossible for historians to quantify. It was known to be so prevalent that a very worried France in 1645 imported thousands of female prostitutes in an attempt to redirect sailors' sex drives.

WHAT ARE PIECES OF EIGHT?

During the Golden Age of Piracy, silver mined by the Spanish was made into coins known as reales. Pieces of eight were 8-reale coins (commonly called a dollar, peso or duro) with a distinctive number 8 stamped into them. They could be broken into eight pieces for smaller purchases.

Pirates, however, did have a form of male civil partnership known as matelotage, in which one man would name another his inheritor. While this could have been used in romantic relationships, it was more likely applied to master-apprentice relationships, where the sex tended to take the form of abuse between the dominant master and the younger apprentice beholden to him to pay off a debt. Also, since there were so few women available in the pirate world, two men may have formed a matelotage simply to have somebody to leave their earthly belongings to. Once the arrangement ended, a matelot could choose a new partner. Some have speculated that the mariner words "mate" and "matey" derived from matelotage, though most researchers dispute that.

HEALTH INSURANCE

Piracy may seem like the ultimate gig job, but buccaneers did have a form of health insurance— a vital work benefit as the average pirate of the 16th and 17th century was constantly at risk of health and safety catastrophes. Captain Henry Morgan (see page 100) famously drafted a plan that spelled out compensation according to body part. The loss of a right arm would be worth 600 pieces of eight, 500 for a left arm and 1,800 for the loss of both legs. An eye or a finger were each worth 100 pieces. Total blindness got 2,000. To put that in perspective, 2,000 pieces of eight is worth about $150,000 today. If pirates didn't want cash, they could collect it in slaves.

GENDER, RACIAL AND RELIGIOUS TOLERANCE

While not exactly havens of feminism—see the many accounts of violent rapes—pirate ships did offer a slightly more equal work environment for women in an era when females were treated as no better than cattle and property by the law and society. This is evidenced by the famous, if brief, success of 18th-century female pirates Anne

One merchant captain said, "There is so little government and subordination among [pirates], that they are, on occasion, all captains, all leaders."

Bonny and Mary Read (see pages 110–113), who dressed, swore and fought just like the men.

This tolerance extended to race and religion. Pirates essentially didn't care who you were or where you came from as long as you were dedicated to the cause of stealing treasure and wreaking havoc on the high seas. Blackbeard's crew was two-thirds Black—including both escaped and freed slaves—among them his right-hand man, known as Black Caesar.

DEMOCRATIC ELECTIONS

On pirate ships, captains weren't assigned; they were voted in. Though lawbreakers by nature and profession, on their ships the crews had to abide by a strict set of rules and regulations, "articles of agreement" that were uniform throughout the pirate world over the decades.

Among the requirements: Captains were elected by the crew and served at their pleasure, or faced replacement. Their share of booty also was spelled out in advance—usually twice that of a regular pirate, but a considerably smaller cut than those enjoyed by naval and privateer captains. ⚓

TOP-EARNING PIRATES

Forbes magazine dug into the history books, crunched the numbers and decided that Samuel "Black Sam" Bellamy had the highest career earnings of any pirate, some $120 million in today's dollars, much of that from looting along the New England coastline in the 18th century. Second place went to 16th-century British privateer Sir Francis Drake, who plundered $115 million when he wasn't fending off the Spanish Armada for Her Majesty. Meanwhile, one of the most famous pirates, Blackbeard, raked in a relatively modest $12.5 million.

The Battle of New Orleans

Black Bart's final skirmish

Jean Lafitte

The End of an Era

Naval firepower and newfound liberty on land doomed the swashbuckling golden age

After 70 years, the Golden Age of Piracy came to an end around 1720, or so say the history books. No single event doomed the buccaneers and corsairs, although the deaths in battle, or by execution, of the famous captains Blackbeard in 1718, Charles Vane in 1721 and Bartholomew Roberts the following year, along with the hangings of their crews, sent a message of deterrence that finally seemed to resonate.

Privateers still flourished afterward, during both the American and French revolutions and in the War of 1812, and an enterprising pirate like

Blackbeard's last stand

HOW A CIVIL WAR "PIRATE" INSPIRED *GONE WITH THE WIND*'S AUTHOR

During the American Civil War, the Confederate States called on privateers to attack Union ships, capture its merchant vessels and seize their cargoes, in the hopes of ending the U.S. Navy's blockade of Southern ports. The exploits of one of the "pirates," George Trenholm, later inspired *Gone With the Wind* author Margaret Mitchell, who based the character of Rhett Butler on the shipping and banking magnate who served as the treasurer of the Confederacy in 1865, during the last year of the Civil War. Trenholm masterminded the South's blockade-running efforts, smuggling cotton and gold out of the country to buy medicines and ammunition in Europe, but he also brought in luxuries like silk slippers and brocade fabrics that he sold for a fortune. He was imprisoned after the war for treason, but was pardoned by President Andrew Johnson. Mitchell described her protagonist, played by Clark Gable (right) in the 1939 film, as "dark of face, swarthy as a pirate."

Jean Lafitte—who captured and traded in slaves from his base on an island south of New Orleans—could still make a living as an outlaw of the sea.

But after becoming an unlikely hero during the War of 1812, when he helped General Andrew Jackson fight off British ships in the Battle of New Orleans, Lafitte's return to piracy came to an end when a U.S. warship in 1821 burned his Galveston Island fortress to the ground and sent him fleeing. He was believed to have died two years later.

The privateering racket began to dry up when one former Spanish colony after another—Mexico, Peru, Chile, Ecuador, Colombia and Venezuela, all countries that relied on privateers against Spain—liberated themselves.

Only Cuba remained under Spanish control, and there, from the northern coast, pirates found refuge and launched raids on American ships laden with cargo from the booming Industrial Revolution.

But the crews were now smaller and the prizes more meager—one U.S. captain reported that in one raid, pirates got away with little more than $16, some pots and pans, and a compass—and resistance was fierce. As Britain and America prioritized stamping out piracy, by the 1820s, wrote Angus

Konstam in 2008's *Piracy: The Complete History*, "the pirate problem had been almost completely eradicated, and the waters of the Caribbean were once again deemed safe for maritime trade."

Piracy still took place for decades in other areas, most notably in the China Sea and, to this day, off the coast of Somalia, but the golden age was over. Piracy changed because the Western world was changing. The philosophies behind the American and French revolutions declared that even ordinary men have "certain unalienable rights," which meant that "the sea was no longer the only refuge open to the oppressed," author Frank Sherry wrote in his history of the golden age, *Raiders and Rebels*. "And so the great pirate brotherhood—the piracy of the great outbreak, fueled by the hunger for freedom—withered away." ⚓

Modern-Day Marauders

Automatic weapons have replaced cutlasses, but young men still turn to piracy for the same reasons

I t was only a small fishing boat, but it spoke to a larger concern. The captors who seized the craft off the coast of Somalia in January 2018 likely planned to use it as a "mother ship" to launch further attacks, promising to escalate a problem that governments had thought was under control. One thing was clear: After a steady decline, the pirates were back.

Hundreds of years after the last of the colorful buccaneers of the Golden Age of Piracy were vanquished by naval forces and changing social and economic conditions, piracy still plagues parts of the world, particularly the waters off Somalia and Nigeria.

"Governments just don't have the capability of going out and addressing this problem.... They don't have enough vessels."

**PROFESSOR BRANDON PRINS,
THE UNIVERSITY OF
TENNESSEE, KNOXVILLE**

"I AM THE CAPTAIN NOW"

In 2013's *Captain Phillips*, Tom Hanks (above) once again played an everyman hero—portraying the real-life Captain Richard Phillips, who offered himself as a hostage to save his crew after his container ship was boarded by Somali pirates for ransom in April 2009. Hanks told *The Wall Street Journal* that the film shined a light on why young men today would turn to piracy. "There's this underlying hopelessness because of the geopolitics of what a disaster Somalia has become," he said.

As for the real Captain Phillips, the ordeal—ending in his rescue by the U.S. Navy—speaks to what occurs when the inevitable happens. As he said in an interview with *Parade* magazine: "I always told my crew it wasn't a matter of *if*, it was a matter of *when*."

Pirates today look very much like they did in centuries gone by. They're mostly young men, often fishermen or former soldiers, motivated by the same factors as their swashbuckling forefathers: poverty; lack of social and economic opportunities; and war and civil unrest at home. The sea offers benefits they can't find on land—but unlike the pirates of old, their punishments are often relatively light, with many treated as heroes in their villages, which enjoy economic benefits from their piracy. The days of public hangings are long over.

Operating from bases in countries with weak or corrupt governments that can't—or won't—crack down on them, the pirates kidnap fishermen and capture oil tankers, then seek large ransom payments. Modern piracy reached a peak in 2010 when Somali pirates hijacked 49 ships and seized more than 1,000 hostages.

Shipping companies fought back by beefing up security, installing anti-boarding barriers and staying within the safest, most heavily patrolled sea lanes. In 2016, there were no recorded kidnappings in the so-called High Risk Area in the Indian Ocean. But as crews became more complacent, and captains started taking shortcuts through more dangerous waters, the number of attacks and their severity grew alarmingly.

"The increase in kidnap and ransom attacks is troubling, as they tend to entail greater violence," Maisie Pigeon, co-author of a report by nonprofit organization Oceans Beyond Piracy, told CNN in January 2018. "They involve less risk to the pirates themselves and can produce lucrative returns."

In 2020, attacks were up by 20 percent, according to the International Maritime Bureau.

PHANTOM SHIPS

Modern-day pirates don't just take hostages and demand ransoms—some sea-jackings involve stealing ships and re-documenting them to appear legitimate. One notable case, in 1990, involved an Australian cargo freighter—the *Erria Inge*—which disappeared near Bedi, India, while carrying a shipment of soybeans months after it was chartered by a Chinese company. The owner of the ship and the company lost contact with the ship and the crew, and it was later learned that it had been given a new name—the *Hai Sin*—and fake papers, allowing it to be used in legal shipping as a phantom ship. The story took a more macabre turn when it was bought as scrap and the remains of 10 burned and decomposing bodies were discovered in an unused freezer.

> *"[Nigerian pirates] move fast, take part in ferocious gun battles and snatch victims off ships before retreating into the Niger Delta's maze of rivers."*
>
> **THE ECONOMIST**

Along with a boost in Somalian piracy, ship attacks and kidnappings surged off the west coast of Africa. Governments and ship owners have responded with more security and more patrols, but the issues run deeper. As long as there are economic and political problems on land, the troubles will continue in the seas. ⚓

UNDER ATTACK

THREE OF THE MOST INFAMOUS MODERN RAIDS

DECEMBER 2001

Noted New Zealand sailor Sir Peter Blake was sailing up the Amazon as part of a research expedition aboard the yacht *Seamaster* when eight armed pirates boarded his ship while anchored outside the Brazilian city of Macapá. Blake shot one of the intruders and was killed as the attackers fled.

NOVEMBER 2009

Somali pirates northeast of the Seychelles seized the Greek-flagged tanker *Maran Centaurus*, carrying 2 million barrels of oil. The 28 crew members were held for nearly two months until a ransom of $7 million was dropped from an aircraft. The crew was released, but two of the pirates were killed in a gun battle with a rival gang.

FEBRUARY 2011

Somali pirates captured the American yacht *SY Quest* off the coast of Oman, holding four U.S. citizens for ransom. After a rocket grenade was fired toward a U.S. warship, Navy rescuers boarded the yacht and two pirates were killed. All four captives were found dead, apparently killed by the pirates. The rest of the pirates surrendered.

NOVEMBER 2020

Piracy continues to be a brisk business in the Gulf of Guinea, off Nigeria. By the end of the month, there were 23 kidnappings with 118 abductees, according to maritime security company Dryad Global. The area was given a "critical risk" rating with crews on high alert.

CHAPTER 2

BATTLES AND SHIPS

*Pirates sailed the open seas in search
of bounty, booty and easy prey.
Here's how they (mostly) got the job done*

Ships That Sailed

Pirate vessels were fast, sleek, heavily armed, packed with men—and stolen

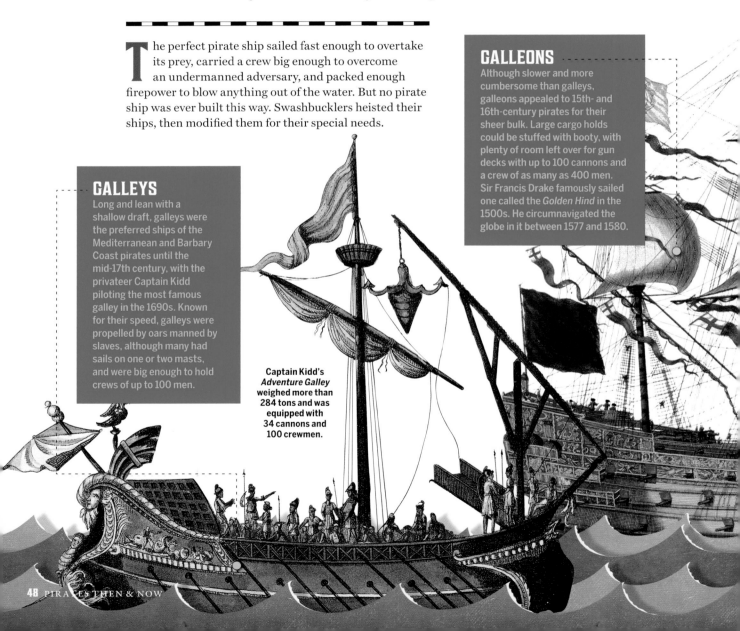

The perfect pirate ship sailed fast enough to overtake its prey, carried a crew big enough to overcome an undermanned adversary, and packed enough firepower to blow anything out of the water. But no pirate ship was ever built this way. Swashbucklers heisted their ships, then modified them for their special needs.

GALLEYS

Long and lean with a shallow draft, galleys were the preferred ships of the Mediterranean and Barbary Coast pirates until the mid-17th century, with the privateer Captain Kidd piloting the most famous galley in the 1690s. Known for their speed, galleys were propelled by oars manned by slaves, although many had sails on one or two masts, and were big enough to hold crews of up to 100 men.

GALLEONS

Although slower and more cumbersome than galleys, galleons appealed to 15th- and 16th-century pirates for their sheer bulk. Large cargo holds could be stuffed with booty, with plenty of room left over for gun decks with up to 100 cannons and a crew of as many as 400 men. Sir Francis Drake famously sailed one called the *Golden Hind* in the 1500s. He circumnavigated the globe in it between 1577 and 1580.

Captain Kidd's *Adventure Galley* weighed more than 284 tons and was equipped with 34 cannons and 100 crewmen.

the Seven Seas

The *Golden Hind* remained docked for public visitations until 1650, before it rotted. A replica (called the *Golden Hinde*) is still on view in London today.

PERIAGUAS

Used for quick raids by Caribbean pirates, these were generally small, fast, silent, light boats that were rowed, but often also fitted with a sail. Using stealth and surprise, these boats could overtake larger sloops and barques. Inspired by boats used by indigenous people, periaguas ranged from small dugout canoes that fit a couple of people, to craft that held a crew of 45 men.

Captains Benjamin Hornigold and "Black Sam" Bellamy began their pirate careers on periaguas.

WHO'S THE LADY ON THE BOW?

Like most sailors, pirates believed that it was bad luck to have a woman on a ship. The exception was a wood carving of a woman, often scantily clad, on the bow. Called figureheads, they gazed out from the fronts of ships for centuries, from the warships of the ancient Phoenicians and Greeks through the sloops and schooners of the Golden Age of Piracy. Superstitious mariners believed female figureheads warded off evil spirits, or pleased the gods of the seas and heavens. The sculptures served practical purposes, too, helping nearly universally illiterate sailors identify ships and—if the figure was sexy enough—to distract adversaries in battle. Expensive to produce and so heavy they slowed ships, sailors stopped using them in the 1800s.

XEBECS

Favored among Barbary pirates, these ships were similar to galleys in that they had both oars and sails, although they were larger, with up to 40 cannons and 400 crewmen. Recognizable by their pronounced overhanging bow and stern, xebecs had a narrow floor but a fat beam to carry up to three masts with sails that could be close-hauled for maximum speed.

Xebecs were not designed for rough seas and bad weather, so they were better suited to the Mediterranean than the Caribbean.

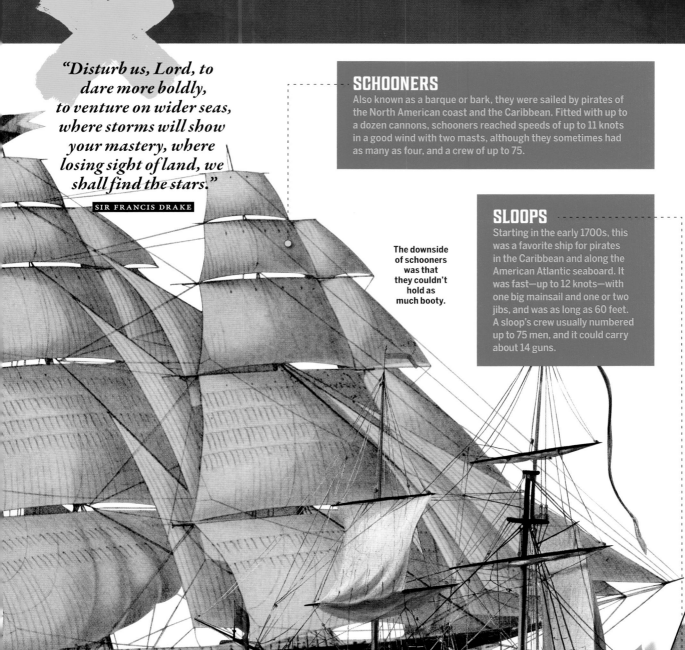

> *"Disturb us, Lord, to dare more boldly, to venture on wider seas, where storms will show your mastery, where losing sight of land, we shall find the stars."*
> **SIR FRANCIS DRAKE**

SCHOONERS

Also known as a barque or bark, they were sailed by pirates of the North American coast and the Caribbean. Fitted with up to a dozen cannons, schooners reached speeds of up to 11 knots in a good wind with two masts, although they sometimes had as many as four, and a crew of up to 75.

The downside of schooners was that they couldn't hold as much booty.

SLOOPS

Starting in the early 1700s, this was a favorite ship for pirates in the Caribbean and along the American Atlantic seaboard. It was fast—up to 12 knots—with one big mainsail and one or two jibs, and was as long as 60 feet. A sloop's crew usually numbered up to 75 men, and it could carry about 14 guns.

In *Peter Pan*, Captain Hook had a sloop named the *Jolly Roger*. A model of it can be seen at Disneyland in Anaheim, California.

The Jolly Roger's Devilish History

The skull and crossbones brought plenty of terror, but also helped to avoid a battle

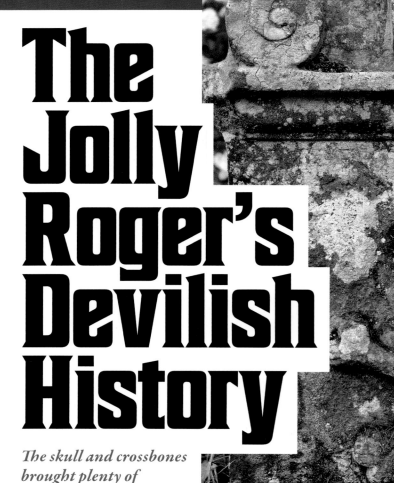

Many old graves, like this one in Scotland, feature tombstones with the skull and crossbones symbol.

Long a symbol of death etched on European tombstones, the skull and crossbones first fluttered on the pirate ship flags known as Jolly Rogers around the late 1600s, and for centuries it sent fear through the hearts of sailors around the world.

When and how these flags came to be called the Jolly Roger is not entirely known. "Old Roger" was a common nickname for the devil, and the term "Jolly Roger" debuted in print in the 1724 book *A General History of the Robberies and Murders of the Most Notorious Pyrates*, which credits captains Bartholomew Roberts and Francis Spriggs with calling their flags Jolly Rogers.

Neither captain's flag contained the skull and crossbones emblem, however, suggesting that Jolly Roger was a generic term for any pirate flag design, of which there were many.

Henry Every fashioned an aristocratic-looking flag of four gold chevrons on a red background. Blackbeard, Richard Worley, Howell Davis and Charles Vane all flew plain black flags. (See page 55 for more on these flags.)

The first recorded use of the skull and crossbones by a pirate was in 1687—on a red flag that was planted on land, not on the bow of a ship. Thirteen years later, a British Navy ship captain made the first recorded sighting of a nautical pirate's flag when he described "crossbones, a death's head and an hourglass" above pirate leader Emanuel Wynn's ship at the Cape Verde islands off West Africa.

Ships' flags had numerous logos depending on the pirate captain's artistic—and sadistic—sensibilities. Many included an hourglass to warn their prey that time was running out. Others added daggers and spears and dripping hearts. Some had two skulls or an entire skeleton.

The traditional skull and crossbones against a black backdrop first started appearing in the 1710s above the ships of Edward England, John Taylor and "Black Sam" Bellamy. By the 1720s, it had become the most popular design throughout the Caribbean, Atlantic seaboard and Indian Ocean.

The "pirate's brand," as modern-day researchers call it, did not fly at all times. Pirates instead usually sailed under fake colors until they were upon their prey, then they would unfurl the pirate flag, often to the accompaniment of a nerve-jarring cannon shot.

This was to identify themselves as pirates, rather than military vessels, to give their targets a chance to respond accordingly—namely, to surrender. As Tom Wareham, who was the curator of maritime history at the Museum of London Docklands, told *The New York Times*, "What pirates wanted was profit, and to make it in the least costly way without wasting time and ammunition attacking a ship and taking lots of casualties."

If a targeted captain refused to back down, the Jolly Roger would come down and a red flag would go up, signaling in dire terms an attack was imminent, and no mercy would be shown. ⚓

In 1945, British officers displayed the Jolly Roger with symbols for five ships torpedoed or sunk by gunfire in the U-Boat war.

The Jolly Roger flies on the Royal Navy's HMS *Splendid* ahead of its decommission in 2004.

WHY SUBMARINES FLY THE JOLLY ROGER

Beginning in World War I, British submariners adopted the skull and crossbones flag as their symbol in irreverent memory of First Sea Lord Admiral Sir Arthur Wilson: He had compared submarine warfare to piracy, griping that subs were "underhanded, unfair, and damned un-English." This naval tradition grew in popularity during World War II, as the U.K. and Allied Forces flew the Jolly Roger to signal successful missions; the practice continues to this day. In 2017, the U.S. Navy attack submarine USS *Jimmy Carter* was photographed returning home from a voyage flying the pirate flag. Since the sub specializes in top-secret missions, the nature of the victory remained classified.

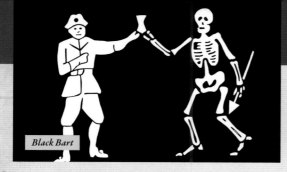

Black Bart

Henry Every

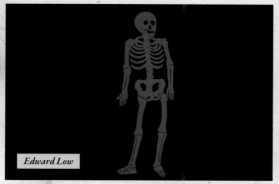

Edward Low

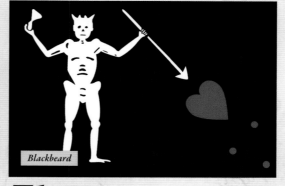

Blackbeard

Fancy Flags

The Jolly Roger reflects a captain's artistic—and sadistic—tastes, but not all marauders flew the skull and crossbones, preferring their own designs.

What do you call a pirate who didn't fly the skull and crossbones flag? Still a pirate. While these rogues of the sea have been associated with the ominous black-and-white flag since the 1600s, many flaunted their own devilish versions. The very name "Jolly Roger," first recorded in print in 1724, likely applied to any pirate flag, no matter the design or color, though the intentions were always the same: to instill fear in targeted vessels to force surrender. Here are what some pirates chose to hoist instead.

FAKE FLAGS

Many pirates delayed flying their signature flags for as long as possible, instead sailing in disguise under false colors until they were close to their prey. Then they would unfurl the pirate flag, often to the accompaniment of a cannon shot.

BARTHOLOMEW "BLACK BART" ROBERTS

One of the most successful pirates of all time, based on the number of boats raided—some 400—Roberts changed flags over his career, but both had one thing in common: images of himself. His first flag showed Black Bart next to the figure of Death holding an hourglass, a common pirate symbol warning prey that their time was running out. A later flag also featured Roberts, only this time he was standing on two skulls.

HENRY EVERY

The pirate responsible for the single biggest raid in history appears to have shunned bones, skulls or images of death altogether on his flag. Rather, it is said that he fashioned an aristocratic-looking flag of four gold chevrons against a red background. This is according to the ballad "A Copy of Verses," which is not an entirely accurate source, but at least it's the only one available. Although many picture black backgrounds as standard for pirate flags, red was just as popular.

EDWARD LOW

The notorious pirate of the American Northeast flew one of the most famous flags of the Golden Age of Piracy, a red skeleton against a black background. Later, he is also said to have used a silk flag with a yellow figure of a man blowing a trumpet against a green background, which was flown on the mizzen peak to summon captains of his fleet to his ship, or the flagship.

BLACKBEARD

The flag many link to Edward Teach, aka Blackbeard, features a skeleton with horns piercing a bleeding heart with a spear, though there are no contemporaneous accounts to confirm this design. Instead, he's described as flying black flags or "bloody flags," and many believe it could have been as simple as black fabric with no design.

Hideouts & Havens

The safe ports the buccaneers, corsairs, cutthroats and thieves called home

BARATARIA BAY, LOUISIANA

French smuggler Jean Lafitte acted as the head of a pirate syndicate, trading in slaves and valuables—taken from Spanish ships—on a bustling black-market island in the bay. Lafitte later took sides with the United States and became a hero of the War of 1812 in the Battle of New Orleans, receiving a full presidential pardon for his previous misdeeds.

PORT ROYAL, JAMAICA

Known as the "wickedest city on Earth," this lawless Caribbean port offered gambling, drinking and the opportunity to "crack Jenny's teacup," pirate slang for a night with a prostitute. Sir Henry Morgan holed up here, though the straight-laced seaman reportedly refused to partake in the town's many pleasures.

NEW PROVIDENCE, BAHAMAS

Strategically located in the sea lanes between the West Indies and Europe, this Caribbean island welcomed the likes of Blackbeard and Charles Vane with drink and women—along with safe harborage—until the British Crown chased out the pirate population with a combination of pardons and executions in the early 1700s.

TORTUGA ISLAND, HAITI

French hunters expelled by Spain in the early 1600s relocated to this rugged island off the coast of Hispaniola and sailed out of a harbor guarded by a castle with 24 cannons, launching revenge raids on their Spanish tormentors.

SALÉ, MOROCCO

Daniel Defoe's tale of Robinson Crusoe as being kidnapped by, then escaping from, Salé Rovers is based on this real-life self-styled republic at the mouth of the Bou Regreg River in modern-day western Morocco.

"The popular image of lawless havens of prostitutes, alcoholism and squalor is not one far from the truth."

NICK SMITH,
AUTHOR OF
ROGUES' NEST

ST. MARY'S ISLAND, MADAGASCAR

A pirate's paradise, this island off the African coast offered secluded inlets for Captain Kidd and his ilk to repair and restock their ships between attacks on Indian Ocean ships loaded with gold, jewels and exotic goods from India. Rogue American merchants came to trade for the booty, and the most successful swashbucklers "retired" here to lives of leisure with multiple wives.

The Art of War

Seven of the most dramatic skirmishes in pirate history

SIR FRANCIS DRAKE VS. THE *CONCEPCION*

YEAR 1579

LOCATION Around Esmeraldas, Ecuador

Queen Elizabeth I's favorite privateer sneaked his ship, the *Golden Hind*, up to the massive Spanish galleon *Nuestra Señora de la Concepción* under cover of darkness, unleashed a broadside (fired all the guns on one side of the ship), and boarded with virtually no resistance, hauling off so much gold and silver it took six days to unload. When he brought the treasure back to England, the queen knighted him.

HENRY EVERY VS. MUGHAL FLAGSHIP

YEAR 1695

LOCATION Arabian Sea

Between modern-day Yemen and Surat, India, English pirate Henry Every's 46-cannon frigate, named *Fancy*, attacked the 80-cannon Mughal flagship, *Ganj-i-Sawai*—the largest ship of India—in a bloody raid. Every's men tortured the crew and raped the women passengers over several days before taking off with gold, silver and exotic goods worth tens of millions of dollars today.

CAPTAIN MORGAN INVADES PANAMA

YEAR 1671

LOCATION Old Panama City, Panama

Under a privateer license from the English government, Captain Henry Morgan and 300 crewmen landed on the Atlantic side of Panama, crossed the isthmus and routed 1,600 Spanish troops, then spent weeks raping, torturing and plundering—before loading up 175 pack animals with treasure and burning down the town.

CAPTAIN KIDD BECOMES A PIRATE

YEAR 1698

LOCATION Somewhere in the Indian Ocean

In the raid that got William Kidd branded a pirate, the Scottish sailor took over the Armenian-run cargo ship *Quedagh Merchant* and sailed her to the Caribbean, selling some of the booty and burying the rest before setting the ship ablaze and sinking it off the coast of the present-day Dominican Republic. The wreck was discovered in 2007.

'CALICO' JACK RACKHAM VS. SPANISH GUNBOAT

YEAR 1720 **LOCATION** Cuba

While the English pirate was in Cuba getting his ship repaired, a Spanish gunship and a captured English sloop anchored in a harbor entrance, waiting to attack him at morning high tide. But that night, Rackham and his crew quietly rowed out, fought off the Spanish guards and stealthily took off in their sloop, while the gunboat pounded Rackham's empty ship.

BLACKBEARD BLOCKADES CHARLESTON

YEAR 1718

LOCATION Charleston Harbor, North Carolina

The most audacious operation by the notorious pirate came when he blockaded the entrance to Charleston's harbor with his mighty ship, *Queen Anne's Revenge*. After looting several ships of cargo and taking women captive, he ransomed the town in exchange for a chest of medicine for the hostages.

SOMALI PIRATES VS. THE MV *SIRIUS STAR*

YEAR 2008 **LOCATION** Off the coast of southeast Kenya

The largest ship ever commandeered by pirates, the 1,000-foot-long supertanker MV *Sirius Star* of Saudi Arabia, worth $150 million and carrying $100 million in oil, was hijacked by Somali pirates who held her for more than two months before releasing the ship and her crew of 25 for a ransom of $3 million. ⚓

Attack Mode

Weapons in the Golden Age of Piracy ranged from knives and guns to mighty cannons

Swivel cannon

Boarding ax

Deck cannon

While the elements of fear and surprise were handy ammunition in the pirates' arsenal, they also had a collection of lethal weapons to choose from.

DECK CANNON

By the Golden Age of Piracy, ships carried up to 100 massive cast-iron cannons in a variety of sizes that were capable of firing ammunition weighing from 6 to 32 pounds. These mighty guns, themselves weighing from 600 to 5,000 pounds, were mounted on the sides of ships on small ramps, and secured with heavy breech ropes and side tackle. Under the command of a master gunner, the crews fired fixed loads inserted into the muzzle to improve accuracy (and avoid mishaps). With such heavy strain from the blasts, the guns only lasted for 500 to 1,000 shots until they had to be replaced.

SWIVEL CANNON

Mounted on a swiveling stand and loaded through the muzzle, this smallest of the cannons fired grapeshot (a collection of small cannonballs packed into a canvas bag) from short range at targeted crewmen. Though not powerful enough to disable or sink a ship, swivel cannons were relatively light and portable, and could be carried to different locations on the ship. The small cannonballs could be used to take out massed infantry—and were also large enough to puncture sails and cut rigging.

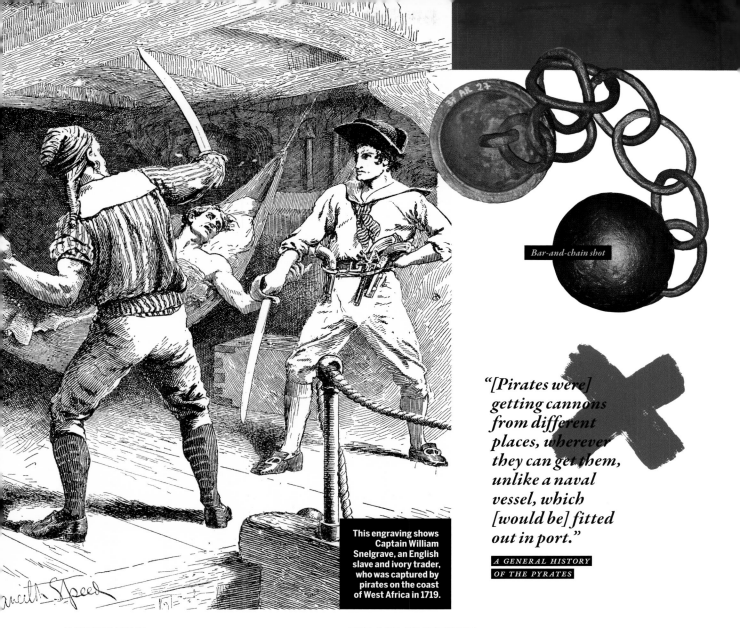

Bar-and-chain shot

This engraving shows Captain William Snelgrave, an English slave and ivory trader, who was captured by pirates on the coast of West Africa in 1719.

"[Pirates were] getting cannons from different places, wherever they can get them, unlike a naval vessel, which [would be] fitted out in port."

A GENERAL HISTORY OF THE PYRATES

CANNON SHOT

Heavy balls, or round shot, fit loosely into the cannons and weren't accurate, especially in pitching seas, so they were usually fired from close range singularly or in a devastating broadside attack (where all the guns on one side of the ship are fired together). Because of their heavy size, they could inflict major damage, downing tall masts, wiping out rudders and sinking entire ships.

BAR-AND-CHAIN SHOT

These were two cannonballs attached by a chain and blasted out of a cannon to destroy rigging and sails. Only accurate and effective at close range, they would do little damage to ships' hulls.

SANGRENEL

A cloth bag filled with anything sharp and nasty—scrap iron or glass—would be fired out of a cannon

Musket

> *"The pyrate fired a broadside, charged with all manner of small shot. A fatal stroke to them!"*

This 1812 engraving shows swivel cannons being used to fire at a ship in a bay.

from short range to inflict maximum injury and quickly demoralize opponents, as it would take a long, painful time to extract the shrapnel.

EXPLOSIVE SHELL

To add extra punch, hollowed-out cannonballs would be filled with gunpowder, their fuses lit, and then they'd be fired at a ship, exploding upon impact. Other cannonballs would be heated up to red-hot and blasted at a ship to set it ablaze. Both tactics required impeccable timing and posed serious risk to the gun crews.

BELAYING PIN

Normally used to secure ropes (called lines on ships), these heavy, solid wood or metal objects with round handles and cylindrical shafts came in handy as clubs during hand-to-hand combat.

BOARDING AX

With a sharp blade on one side and a heavy hammer on the other, these tomahawk-like weapons with 2- to 3-foot-long handles could break away rigging, chop down masts and rip

through doors and hatches to get to hidden treasure—to say nothing of the damage they could inflict on a human being. They also served defensive purposes, clearing away downed rigging and dislodging smoldering cannonballs from the woodwork, and helped pirates steady themselves when boarding a large ship from a smaller boat.

MARLINSPIKE

About the size of a railroad spike, the marlinspike was made of wood or metal and served multiple nautical purposes, from opening up crates to untangling ropes. Usually carried in leather

Grenado

Flintlock pistol

Dagger

Most pistols only fired a single shot, so pirates carried more than one.

boarding operations, hacking through man and rigging alike on top decks and being small enough for cramped below-deck fighting.

DAGGER

Virtually all sailors carried some sort of small multipurpose knife for routine tasks on the ship and even for eating. The dagger doubled as an effective weapon because the crossbar (or hilt) at its handle protected the hand from a slashing enemy cutlass. Used skillfully, the dagger would clank away the cutlass, then be wielded in counterattack.

FLINTLOCK PISTOL

Due to their compact size and relatively light weight, these weapons were popular among pirates during boarding raids and for walking-around protection. Because the pistols fired only one shot and took a long time to load through the muzzle, pirates carried multiple guns—Blackbeard had three of them strapped to his chest at all times, and Bartholomew Roberts carried at least four—and only used them in close combat, since they were inaccurate from a distance.

MUSKET

Operating the same way as the pistols, muzzle-loading flintlock muskets replaced the less-reliable (especially in rain and high seas) matchlock rifles and served as sniper guns, firing on opposing ships from longer range; however, they were too long and cumbersome for close fighting.

GRENADO

Forerunners to modern hand grenades, these deadly weapons were little more than glass balls filled with gunpowder and projectiles, like iron and glass shards, with a fuse attached. They could be unpredictable and prone to misfiring (or blowing up too early) and were unreliable in wet conditions because the fuses needed to stay dry. But when they worked, they could maim or kill many men and inflict widespread damage. ⚓

pouches by crewmen, marlinspikes also made for effective weapons during battle, since one end was blunted like a club and the other was as sharp as a knife.

CUTLASS

One of the weapons most associated with pirates, this short saber with a curved blade and solid handguard worked well in close combat during

Famous Shipwrecks

It's taken centuries to find long-lost gold, silver and gems

Bellamy's *Whydah Gally* was said to be holding the treasure of 53 other ships, prompting people to flock to the shore looking for treasure after it was wrecked.

What the sea takes it does not easily give back. After hundreds of years, these treasure-laden ships, sunk by nature or man, finally reveal themselves to fortune hunters, though the biggest riches may come from the knowledge gleaned about times gone by.

SAMUEL BELLAMY'S *WHYDAH GALLY*

The first positively identified pirate shipwreck ever recovered, the remains of Samuel "Black Sam" Bellamy's vessel eluded treasure hunters for more than 260 years. For guidance, underwater explorer

Barry Clifford pored over vintage charts, including a map of the wreck site made in 1717, shortly after the *Whydah Gally* went down during a fierce nor'easter off the coast of Cape Cod, Massachusetts. What was surprising was how close the wreck site had been all these years: Clifford found the *Whydah* in 1984, just a few hundred yards offshore beneath only 14 feet of water and 5 feet of sand.

Regular retrieval missions have brought up a wealth of artifacts. The biggest find was the ship's bell inscribed with "THE WHYDAH GALLY 1716" that offered confirmation of the wreck's

and Buried Treasure

Palmyra Atoll

identity. As for treasure, the expectation was that a bounty existed under the sea, and Clifford was not disappointed. Bellamy was one of the most successful pirates in history, with a total haul worth $120 million in today's money, including millions of dollars in gold and silver, some 600 bracelets, as well as other jewelry and objects.

In 1988, the Massachusetts Supreme Court ruled that under maritime law, Clifford could keep all of the items recovered from the *Whydah*. He has maintained most of the collection at a private facility where researchers can study the treasures and learn more about life on a pirate ship. The general public can view selected items at Clifford's Whydah Pirate Museum in West Yarmouth, Massachusetts. He also retains exclusive dive rights to the site, which is patrolled by the National Park Service and the U.S. Coast Guard.

BLACKBEARD'S *QUEEN ANNE'S REVENGE*

When underwater scavengers located a shipwreck off the coast of North Carolina in 1996, excitement built that one of the most famous pirate ships in history, Edward "Blackbeard" Teach's flagship

THE LOST TREASURE OF THE INCAS

The most remote spot with buried treasure may be on the Palmyra Atoll, a dot of land in the middle of the Pacific Ocean about 1,000 miles south of Hawaii. It was here in 1816 that a Spanish pirate ship, the *Esperanza*, with a cargo of gold, silver and gems looted from Inca temples, smashed into a coral reef. The treasure was buried and the ship repaired, and most of the 90 crewmen sailed away. Ten men remained, barely surviving for a year before six of them ventured off in a boat, which was found by a whaler. All but one of them died before reaching land. The last man, James Hines, died in a hospital a month later—but not before writing letters revealing the location of the treasure. The letters wouldn't surface for more than 100 years, but the cache would never be discovered.

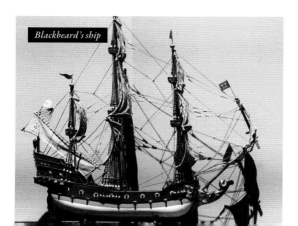

Blackbeard's ship

Queen Anne's Revenge, had finally been found. It was certainly in the right spot, near where the feared pirate captain had run the ship aground on a sandbar in 1718 off Beaufort, a few months before he was killed in battle. It also was large enough to be the *Queen Anne's Revenge*, a 200-ton ship likely built in Bristol, England, in 1710, for merchant service. French privateers seized the ship for several years before Blackbeard captured her in 1717 and renamed her *Queen Anne's Revenge*.

Gold spoon

Gold bar

More than 40 tons of silver and gold was found on the *Nuestra Señora de Atocha* as well as jewelry and 100,000 silver coins.

Silver bar

Gold and emerald cross

"I love to see a wide-eyed child stare at a gold doubloon in wonder and take an interest in its history.... The fascination of lost treasure still has appeal."

TREASURE HUNTER MEL FISHER'S DAUGHTER, TAFFI FISHER ABT

Discovered in 28 feet of water a mile offshore from Fort Macon State Park, the wreck had 31 cannons, which correlated with a well-defended pirate ship. It was the large amount of weaponry that finally confirmed her identity in 2011.

"There was not one aha moment," Claire Aubel of the North Carolina Maritime Museums said at the time of identification. "There was a collection of moments and a deduction based on the evidence." This also included apothecary weights, probably used by the ship's surgeon, stamped with the fleur-de-lis, the royal arms of France, which would align with the ship's use by France as a slave trader.

CAPTAIN KIDD'S *QUEDAGH MERCHANT*

For centuries, all treasure hunters knew was that "Captain" William Kidd had anchored his recently seized ship, the *Quedagh Merchant*, in 1699 in a lagoon somewhere near Santa Catalina Island in the Dominican Republic while he raced back to New York to hide his treasure and clear his name. A privateer licensed to seize French vessels, Kidd had nabbed the *Quedagh Merchant*, an Armenian ship sailing under French protection in 1698, but had the misfortune of discovering the captain was an Englishman, which meant that Kidd was set up for piracy charges.

Jailed when he returned to the American colonies, Kidd refused to disclose the location of the ship and was later hanged for piracy, his secret apparently dying with him. In fact, most of the valuables were sold and the ship burned, and for generations, the location remained a mystery. It was discovered in 2007 by a local resident only 70 feet off the shore of Santa Catalina in just 10 feet of water.

The wreck site is now managed by researchers from Indiana University. "I've been on literally thousands of shipwrecks in my career," said Charles Beeker, PhD, of the university's Center for Underwater Science. "This is one of the first sites I've been on where I haven't seen any looting. We've got a shipwreck in crystal clear, pristine water that's amazingly untouched."

The site is set to become a "Living Museum in the Sea," which will allow the public to explore the wreck and interact with centuries-old artifacts. Alas, you'll need to leave all the treasure behind.

NUESTRA SEÑORA DE ATOCHA

The rearguard ship in a large Spanish convoy, the treasure galleon *Nuestra Señora de Atocha*—Our Lady of Atocha—was loaded with gold, silver, gemstones, copper and indigo from ports in Cuba, Colombia and Panama when the fleet got caught in a hurricane in 1622 in the Florida Keys. The *Atocha* sank in more than 50 feet of water, and all but five of the 265 people on board were killed.

When word reached Spain, a dangerous salvage operation was launched to find the *Atocha* and her sister ship, the *Santa Margarita*. A slave would be put into a brass diving bell with a window and lowered to the sea floor to look for the wreck. The practice killed many slaves and yielded no sign of the *Atocha*, though the *Santa Margarita* was found. Without the *Atocha*'s treasure, Spain had to sell galleons to raise money for the Thirty Years' War, which lasted from 1618 to 1648.

In 1969, after a 16-year search that yielded only a few silver bars and some cannons, a team of treasure hunters led by Mel Fisher discovered the *Atocha* and her treasure—some 40 tons of gold and silver and 71 pounds of emeralds worth hundreds of millions of dollars. (One ring alone was estimated to be worth $500,000.) Fisher showed off another big find, a waist-length heavy gold chain worth as much as $120,000, on *The Tonight Show With Johnny Carson* in 1985.

This windfall did not endear Fisher to the state of Florida, which took the position that it had title to the wreck and that Fisher should hand over 25 percent of the treasure to the state. Fisher fought the dispute all the way to the U.S. Supreme Court, which ruled in his favor in 1992. The haul stands as the most valuable recovered shipwreck in *Guinness World Records*. Laws would subsequently be changed to give states the rights to wrecks within 3 miles of their shorelines.

More than 40 of the items Fisher recovered, including the chain he showed off on *Carson*, were auctioned off in 2015 after his death, fetching a total of $2 million. ⚓

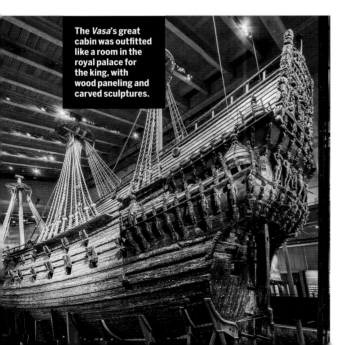

The *Vasa*'s great cabin was outfitted like a room in the royal palace for the king, with wood paneling and carved sculptures.

THE SWEDISH WARSHIP THAT SANK WITHIN MINUTES

It may be the shortest voyage in Swedish naval history. In 1628, the warship *Vasa* set off on her maiden voyage. Built upon orders of the king, she was a magnificent craft, beautifully decorated and heavily armed with brass cannons. But she also suffered a design flaw that left her top-heavy, a problem nobody dared tell the king, who was eager to launch her. After sailing about a quarter mile, a stiff wind caught the *Vasa* and she foundered and sank. Largely forgotten over the centuries, the *Vasa* was discovered in the late 1950s in Stockholm harbor in remarkably good condition, her hull still intact. Divers recovered cannons, coins, tools, cutlery, 10 sails and the remains of at least 15 sailors. The *Vasa* now sits in a museum as one of the most popular tourist attractions in the country.

Pirate Hot Spots You Can See Today

Relive the glory days of sea rovers in these cutthroat havens

Tortuga Channel, Haiti

S ome of the most spectacularly beautiful places on Earth also happen to be rich with buccaneer history. You don't have to fly the Jolly Roger to visit these pirate haunts turned tourist destinations.

TORTUGA, HAITI

Featured in the *Pirates of the Caribbean* franchise—Johnny Depp recruits his crew in the first film in Tortuga and gets dumped there by Barbossa in *At World's End* here—this little island off Haiti was favored by French and British pirates during the 1600s. Also called Turtle Island for its shape (*tortuga* is Spanish for tortoise), the island boasts gorgeous beaches and has plenty of old forts and caves to play pirate. The original corsairs had been French hunters on Haiti who fled for the island to escape Spanish settlers. When they turned to piracy, they protected the island's harbor from the Spanish from the 24-cannon Fort

A tsunami hit Port Royal in 1692

> *"The bustling city of Port Royal literally sank into the harbour in a matter of minutes, remaining perfectly preserved as it was on the day of the earthquake."*
>
> UNESCO WORLD HERITAGE LISTING

Fort de Rocher

St. Mary's Island

de Rocher. The buccaneer fortress was captured by the Spanish in 1654 and now lies in ruins, with only the foundations remaining.

PORT ROYAL, JAMAICA

Charles Vane and "Calico" Jack Rackham holed up in this lawless Caribbean port on the southeastern corner of Jamaica, which became a sort of pirate Las Vegas, known for its gambling halls, taverns and rampant prostitution. Buccaneers would spend their entire share of Spanish loot in just one night on these chaotic streets, where the governors had given the pirates free rein in the 1600s in exchange for protection from Spanish attacks. Port Royal's era of debauchery ended on June 7, 1692, when an earthquake and tsunami buried much of the town under the ocean, killing 2,000 people in what some saw as divine punishment. Town leaders cleared out what was left of the vice and established Gallows

New Providence, Bahamas

in the early 1700s with a combination of pardons and executions. Now the most populous island in the Bahamas and home to the capital city of Nassau, New Providence attracts more than 4 million visitors a year to its pristine beaches, while privacy-minded investors stash their cash in the more than 400 banks and trust companies. While Fort Nassau was demolished in 1897 to make way for a hotel, visitors can step back in time at the Pirates of Nassau museum.

BARATARIA BAY, LOUISIANA

French pirate Jean Lafitte operated his illicit syndicate trading in slaves and valuables taken from Spanish ships in this busy black-market on an island just south of New Orleans. At its peak in

Point, where many a pirate—including Vane and Rackham—were hanged. Today, visitors can tour the well-preserved underwater ruins along with a number of shipwrecks just a few yards offshore.

ST. MARY'S ISLAND

William Kidd, Henry Every and Thomas Tew used this island off the west coast of Madagascar as a rest stop to repair and restock their ships between attacks on Indian Ocean ships. Rogue American merchants from Boston and New York also flocked to the island to trade for that booty. It was here in 1695 that Every hid out after his fleet raided a Mughal ship and took off with $200 million in treasure. Some of the most successful swashbucklers "retired" on St. Mary's Island, with legends telling of a pirate utopia called Libertatia in which they kept their families (including multiple wives). Many of the current inhabitants of St. Mary's Island claim to be descendants of the pirates who lived there.

NEW PROVIDENCE, BAHAMAS

Edward "Blackbeard" Teach and Benjamin Hornigold were among the many famous pirate captains who found safe harbor in this Caribbean island settlement strategically located along the sea lanes between the West Indies and Europe. Control of the town seesawed between the pirates and the Spanish and English colonial powers until the British Crown cleared out the cutthroats

The entrance to Barataria Bay, Louisiana

1853 map

Clew Bay, Ireland

the 1810s, this illegal colony had a population of as many as 1,000 rogues, while pirate ships filled the harbor. Lafitte later took sides with the U.S. and became an unlikely hero of the War of 1812 in the Battle of New Orleans, receiving a full presidential pardon for his previous misdeeds. After the war, however, he returned to his pirate ways. These days, the waters off Barataria Bay offer much friendlier activities in the form of fishing charters.

CLEW BAY, IRELAND

Grace O'Malley and her clan of pirates made the port their home base in the 1500s for raids on English ships and rival clans. The legendary Pirate Queen of Clew Bay defied gender convention as she commanded some 20 ships and hundreds of men, making her the stuff of Irish song and story. Regarded as one of the most beautiful places in Ireland, the remote Clew Bay of Dornish Island was beloved by John Lennon and Yoko Ono—they owned property there and intended to use it as a retreat before the former Beatle was gunned down in 1980. Ono described it as "a place where we thought we could escape the pressures and spend some undisturbed time together."

SALÉ, MOROCCO

In the 17th century, Barbary pirates created the self-governed Republic of Salé in western Morocco. The dreaded Salé Rovers (made famous by Daniel Defoe in *Robinson Crusoe*) sailed out of the port, attacking ships cruising between Europe and colonial destinations. Today, you can tour the city gates that protected the ships as they entered harbor, as well as the Borj Edoumoue, a large fort where captives were held until ransom was paid. ⚓

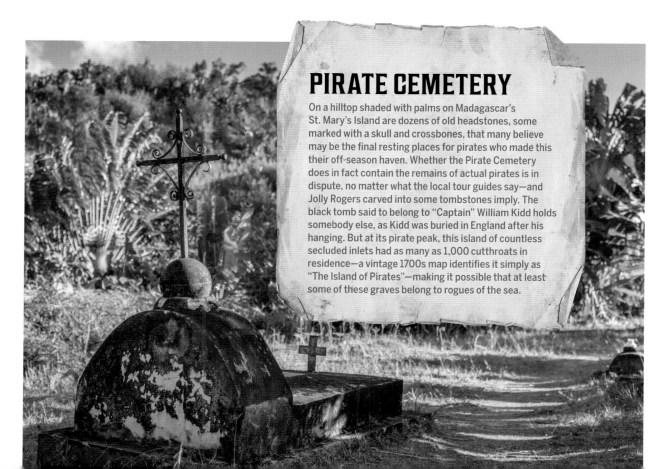

PIRATE CEMETERY

On a hilltop shaded with palms on Madagascar's St. Mary's Island are dozens of old headstones, some marked with a skull and crossbones, that many believe may be the final resting places for pirates who made this their off-season haven. Whether the Pirate Cemetery does in fact contain the remains of actual pirates is in dispute, no matter what the local tour guides say—and Jolly Rogers carved into some tombstones imply. The black tomb said to belong to "Captain" William Kidd holds somebody else, as Kidd was buried in England after his hanging. But at its pirate peak, this island of countless secluded inlets had as many as 1,000 cutthroats in residence—a vintage 1700s map identifies it simply as "The Island of Pirates"—making it possible that at least some of these graves belong to rogues of the sea.

CHAPTER 3

INFAMOUS OUTLAWS

From British knights to former slaves, religious sticklers to noted gourmands, the most famous pirates in history shared a love of adventure—and a thirst for plundering and pillaging

Blackbeard

The smoke coming from Blackbeard's long facial hair made him look "like a frightful meteor," according to a report at the time.

The prototypical buccaneer may have created his evil image to foster fear

As history's most infamous pirate, Blackbeard has inspired everybody from Robert Louis Stevenson to Hollywood producers. Tall and ominous, with three pistols strapped around his chest, Blackbeard was said to have wreathed his hirsute face in smoke smoldering from slow-burning fuses dangling from a fur cap. The effect, one writer said, was a "fury from hell."

Blackbeard was indeed a devil of the sea in the early 1700s, but recent research suggests that his evil persona was manufactured to instill such fear in his targets that violence wasn't necessary. More gentleman than rogue, by all accounts he never killed a single soul, nor inflicted serious damage to another ship, until his final stand 300 years ago. "He likely cultivated that murderous image," archaeologist Charles Ewen of East Carolina University told *Smithsonian* magazine. "Scaring people was a better option than to damage what you are trying to steal."

Believed to have been born Edward Teach (sometimes Thatch or Thache) in 1680 in Bristol, England, he possibly moved with his father, a man of some standing, to Jamaica as a boy. That would have put Edward in high society before he returned to England at about 20, where he either joined the Royal Navy or sailed on privateers—or both—during Queen Anne's War between Britain and France. Near the war's end, he returned to the Caribbean for what would be an illustrious, if brief, life of piracy, starting as second-in-command to notorious buccaneer Captain Benjamin Hornigold.

THE BATTLE OVER HIS WRECK

In 1996, treasure hunters searching the murky waters off Beaufort, North Carolina, found a collection of cannonballs, two anchors, a bronze bell and a sounding weight on the ocean floor. Other discoveries included a book about the South Seas (right). Researchers determined these artifacts came from the final resting spot of Blackbeard's flagship, *Queen Anne's Revenge*, which sank in 1718. More than 300 years after the ship ran aground, shortly before the pirate died in a skirmish, the North Carolina government and a videographer hired by the salvage company had a battle of their own over who owned the valuable rights to videos and photos of the wreck. In early 2020, the U.S. Supreme Court decided in favor of the state, ruling the footage was a matter of public record.

By the fall of 1717, Edward, now a captain, captured the French slave ship *La Concorde*, rechristening her *Queen Anne's Revenge*. Outfitted with 40 cannons, his ship terrorized the Caribbean and Atlantic before heading to South Carolina, where he blockaded the port of Charleston and captured all vessels entering and leaving the harbor.

His career ended—violently—on Nov. 22, 1718, when British naval forces funded by Virginia's governor ambushed Blackbeard's fleet off Ocracoke Island on North Carolina's Outer Banks. The ensuing battle left Blackbeard dead from five gunshot wounds and 20 cuts. His head was propped on a pole overlooking the

"Damn ye, ye yellow-bellied sapsuckers. I'm a better man than all ye milksops put together!"

BLACKBEARD TO HIS MEN, AFTER THEY RAN FROM A FIRE ON THEIR SHIP

Chesapeake in Virginia—at what became known as Blackbeard's Point—as a warning to other pirates who ventured by.

It stayed outside for years, and then one day it disappeared. Local legend had it that a tavern owner took the head and lined the skull

Ian McShane

with silver. He then placed it on display in his Williamsburg, Virginia, tavern, where patrons were dared to drink from it. The skull then reportedly wound up in another bar in the city until the 1950s, when it found its way into the private collection of maritime historian Edward Rowe Snowe.

Snowe took the skull on the road for lectures and when he died, he left it to his widow, who donated it to the Peabody Essex Museum in Salem, Massachusetts. The skull was never authenticated, and only went on display once —the rest of the time, it was stored in the basement, where it gathered a legend as fearsome as the pirate himself. ⚓

Peter Ustinov

BLACKBEARD GETS THE DISNEY TREATMENT

Of all the movie portrayals of the feared pirate, leave it to Disney to feature him in a wacky comedy. *Blackbeard's Ghost* (1968) has a college track coach (Dean Jones) summoning the spirit of the buccaneer, played by Peter Ustinov (above). Because he has to perform one good deed to leave ghostly limbo, Blackbeard helps to save an inn—owned by some elderly ladies—from a bunch of crooks. The movie was a hit with audiences and critics. "Disney's best since *The Absent-Minded Professor*," gushed film critic Roger Ebert. Disney brought back a much more sinister Blackbeard decades later in 2011's *Pirates of the Caribbean: On Stranger Tides*, with Ian McShane (left) donning the dark whiskers.

New exploration of *Queen Anne's Revenge* suggests that Blackbeard wrecked the ship in shallow waters on purpose because it leaked.

Sir Francis Drake

The Englishman made maritime history by circumnavigating the globe

During his voyage of the 1570s, Drake rescued the colonists in the failed settlement of Roanoke, Virginia.

S pain had a special name for its mortal enemy, Sir Francis Drake. It was El Draque—or The Dragon—for the Englishman's seemingly supernatural ability to spot ships on the open water, specifically Spanish ships that Drake would chase down, commandeer and loot. Only a man possessed by the devil, the Spanish believed, could strike with such ruthless efficiency.

At home in England, this son of a tenant farmer —who first sailed as a teenager on his cousin's slave ships—was considered a national treasure and was a favorite of Queen Elizabeth I, who had licensed him as a privateer with the power to raid enemy ships and seize their cargoes.

A near-fatal clash with the Spanish in a Mexican port early in his seagoing career imbued Drake with a lifelong hatred of Spain, which he would manifest by becoming a 16th-century scourge of the Spanish Main, plundering on sea and land and returning to England with riches for his queen.

With England and Spain technically at peace, Elizabeth could not publicly praise him, and for a time he had to go into hiding. In 1577, he set off on his most famous voyage, which took him through the Straits of Magellan off the coast of Chile and around the tip of South America. He lost two ships in storms and tangled with his co-commanders, one of whom Drake had beheaded on mutiny charges.

Drake then plundered the South American coast, made landfall in what is now California, and scored his biggest treasure haul from the Spanish ship, the *Nuestra Señora de la Concepción*, off Ecuador.

Along the way, he circumnavigated the globe, becoming the first Englishman to do so (Ferdinand Magellan was the first person to do it, in 1522, but he was killed by a poison arrow in the Philippines before making it back home to Spain). Drake returned to England after his almost three-year adventure with fabulous riches, a hero's welcome—and a knighthood from a smitten queen who gave him a jewel with her portrait.

Drake later fought the Spanish Armada, elevating him to mythical status in Spain, whose people came to believe he was impossible to kill. So lucky was Drake that during one skirmish a cannonball was said to have sailed between his legs as he stood on deck, leaving him without injury.

He died in 1596 at age 55 of dysentery, sailing off the coast of Panama. Dressed in full armor, he was buried at sea in a lead-lined coffin. Generations of divers have been unable to find his body. ⚓

DRAKE'S GALLEON: THE *GOLDEN HIND*

She was not considered a remarkable ship, but she sure got the job done. The *Golden Hind*, a 120-ton galleon commissioned for Drake for his 1577 voyage, is the ship that took the privateer around the world. Originally christened the *Pelican*, Drake renamed his flagship after his patron, Sir Christopher Hatton, whose family crest was a female red deer, known as a golden hind. The ship was of typical 16th-century design but was fast under sail, highly maneuverable in battle and diminutive enough to hide in small ports. After circumnavigating the globe, the *Golden Hind* was on display for 70 years until it finally decayed. Only a chair carved from its timbers, housed at the University of Oxford, remains. Today, a full-size replica (above, called the *Golden Hinde*), sits on the south bank of the Thames in London.

Queen Elizabeth I knighted Drake aboard his ship in 1581.

Drake dodged a cannonball

Henry Every

*The privateer made the greatest haul of all time
and then disappeared—very, very rich*

He is one of the most successful pirates of all time, and he did it in only two raids. English-born Henry Every (also spelled Avery) sailed for the Royal Navy in battles against the French before he turned privateer as the first officer of the 46-cannon *Charles II*, which prowled the Spanish West Indies for French prizes.

The *Charles II* was an unhappy ship with a drunken captain, and in 1694, when the ship languished in a Spanish port for months without paying the crew, a mutiny erupted, led by Every himself, who informed his woozy commander: "I am captain of this ship now."

The ship was renamed the *Fancy*, and Every set sail for the Indian Ocean in search of the Mughal emperor's fleet as it made the annual pilgrimage to Mecca, the ships filled with pilgrims and a fortune in gold, silver, jewels and other goods.

In 1695, Every joined forces with five other pirate ships and, sitting at the bottleneck strait between the Red Sea and the Gulf of Aden, launched the first raid on the 600-ton escort ship *Fateh Muhammed*, encountering little resistance as the crew scooped up roughly 50,000 pounds in gold and silver.

> *"We with Advice foresaid do make Offer, and Assure the Payment of the Sum of Five Hundred Pounds Sterling for the [capture of] said Henry Every."*
>
> **SCOTTISH PROCLAMATION**

The pirate convoy then attacked the grand prize, the *Ganj-i-Sawai*, the greatest ship of the Mughal Empire, which was carrying a fortune, but was also one of the most heavily protected, with some 400 soldiers and dozens of cannons. After knocking out the ship's mainmast, the pirates stormed the deck and prevailed after a fierce three-hour battle.

After being tortured, crewmen led the pirates to the treasure trove—half a million pieces of gold and silver, along with ivory and other valuables, worth perhaps $200 million today. It was believed to be the single biggest haul; the highest per-capita booty, however, went to the much smaller crew of privateer Thomas Tew's ship, which two years earlier had raided an Arab ship, netting each man a staggering 3,000 pounds in silver, worth $3.5 million today. Still, Every's men were set for life—as was Every, who as a captain got a double share.

As the enraged Grand Mughal Aurangzeb lashed out at his English trading partners, blaming them for the British pirate's crimes, Every and his crew sneaked off to New Providence in the Bahamas. Britain put a bounty on his head, but he managed to slip away into the mists of history, never to be seen again. ⚓

THE MOST VALUABLE BOOTY WASN'T ALWAYS GOLD AND SILVER

Pirates had a plunder list that extended far beyond the usual gold and silver to include food, tools, lumber and hides. One of the most valued targets was a doctor's chest, worth about $470,000 today. So prized was a chest full of curative supplies that when Blackbeard took hostages during the blockade of Charleston, South Carolina, in 1718, he demanded medicine and other medical supplies as ransom.

This illustration shows Captain Henry Every's sloops capturing the *Ganj-i-Sawai*.

Every's exploits inspired songs, books and a play called *The Successful Pyrate*.

Samuel Bellamy

The "Robin Hood of the Sea" robbed the rich—and gave to himself and his crew

Lead shot, spoons, a metal syringe and the crushed barrel of a blunderbuss gun were found on the *Whydah*.

In 1984, treasure hunter Barry Clifford followed a map from 1717 to a spot off the coast of Cape Cod, Massachusetts, where he discovered the remains of a shipwreck under 14 feet of water and 5 feet of sand. The finds included the ship's bell inscribed with "THE WHYDAH GALLY 1716," confirming that this was the flagship of the wealthiest pirate in history, Samuel "Black Sam" Bellamy.

Bellamy spent just over a year as a scoundrel of the seas, but what a year it was. He amassed a fortune worth $120 million today, while earning the reputation among his devoted crew as the "Robin Hood of the Sea," driven by a burning anger toward an English establishment he blamed for exploiting poor rural boys like himself.

Born in Devonshire, England, in 1689, likely to tenant farmers who were perpetually close to starvation, Bellamy joined the Royal Navy as a teen and fought in the War of the Spanish Succession before traveling on a ship to America in 1715.

While serving with pirate captain Benjamin Hornigold, whose first mate was Edward Teach, later to be known as Blackbeard, Bellamy was elected captain in the summer of 1716 by the crew, which was frustrated by Hornigold's refusal to

SAMUEL BELLAMY.

Bellamy famously derided the wealthy as "a pack of crafty rascals" and their ship captains as "hen-hearted numbskulls."

Wax seal from the ship

raid ships from his native England.

Known for his fancy dress and the four ornate dueling pistols tucked into his sash, Bellamy got the nickname "Black" for tying his long, dark hair with a black cord rather than wear the powdered wigs favored by the elites. He was adored by his men for his democratic leadership and aversion to violence.

In 1717, he nabbed the sleek new slave ship *Whydah Gally* and its haul of gold, ivory, indigo and a medicinal tree bark known as "Jesuit's bark." It took only one cannon shot for the *Whydah*'s captain to surrender peacefully, and Bellamy returned the favor by giving him another ship in his fleet.

It was believed that Black Sam never killed a single man and made a point to target the vessels of wealthy English merchants, whom he despised. "They rob the poor under the cover of law, forsooth," he was quoted as saying, "and we plunder the rich under the protection of our own courage."

Making the *Whydah* his flagship, Bellamy sailed for New England to see what he said was his family—but in all likelihood was a teenage beauty with whom he had fathered a child—when a punishing nor'easter sank his ship on April 26, 1717, killing Bellamy and all but two of his 142 men. He was only 29 years old.

After the *Whydah*'s discovery, more than 200,000 pieces of treasure were retrieved, including the ship's bell, cannons and silver coins. They can be seen at the Whydah Pirate Museum in West Yarmouth, Massachusetts. ⚓

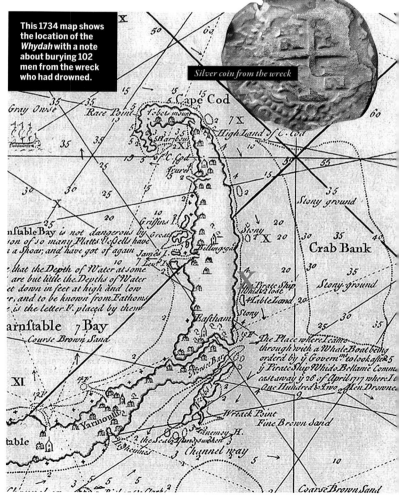

This 1734 map shows the location of the *Whydah* with a note about burying 102 men from the wreck who had drowned.

Silver coin from the wreck

Black Bart drafted rules including what time candles were to be put out (8 o'clock), and instituted the death penalty for any man who smuggled a woman on board.

The Pirate's Code

PIRATA CODEX

Black Bart

Pious only to a point, the captain observed the Sabbath, but was unusually harsh on his men

On Bartholomew "Black Bart" Roberts' ships, musicians were expected to play on demand, 24 hours a day, with only one day off. "The musicians to have rest on the Sabbath Day," read Article XI of Roberts' pirate code, "but the other six days and nights, none without special favour."

Deeply religious, Roberts was a man of contradictions. He created the famous set of pirate rules, adhered to throughout the pirating world, that called for the election of captains, spelled out rules for safety and punishment, and established compensation for injury.

Yet he could be as cruel as any cutthroat, capable of unspeakable acts of violence. In one six-month stretch, Captain Roberts captured at least 100 ships in the Caribbean, including a 52-gun man-of-war carrying Martinique's governor, whom Roberts hanged—but not before torturing and killing the rest of the crew.

Born John Roberts in Wales, he went to sea as early as age 13, and by 1719 rose to second mate of a slave ship captured by pirates off West Africa. The conquering captain, Howell Davis, a fellow Welshman, admired the 37-year-old Roberts' skills as a navigator and made him a confidant.

Although Roberts had no choice but to work on the ship, the life agreed with him; he observed that the "low wages and hard labour" of "honest service" couldn't compete with the "satiety, pleasure and ease, liberty and power" of piracy. "A merry life and a short one shall be my motto," he said.

After Davis was killed in an ambush, the crew elected Roberts captain. He changed his name to the more romantic-sounding Bartholomew and adopted the sinister nickname Black Bart, backing that up by rampaging through the Atlantic Ocean, seizing French, Dutch and English ships and selling them and their cargo on the black market. A pirate for only about three years, Black Bart was killed at the age of 39 when his ship came under fire in 1722 from the British warship HMS *Swallow*. ⚓

A SHARP-DRESSED MAN

Along with being one of the cruelest pirates, Black Bart had the best sense of style. Even in battle, he donned breeches, a crimson waistcoat and a plumed hat. A gold cross, designed for the king of Portugal, hung from his neck, a symbol of his religious beliefs, which influenced how he ran his ship. He refused to fight on Sundays, had a clergyman on board, and barred gambling. But come Monday, it was back to the brutal business of pirating. Black Bart once set fire to a transport ship full of slaves because "unshackling them cost much Time and Labour," according to one written account. Those who didn't burn to death drowned or were eaten by sharks.

William Dampier

While others endured hardtack, this buccaneer enjoyed an epicurean lifestyle

"A dish of flamingo's tongue is fit for a prince's table," Dampier wrote.

I
n his bestselling travel memoir, William Dampier recalled a visit to the Bay of Panama in the late 1600s when he encountered a fruit "as big as large lemon" with "pretty smooth" skin the color of "black bark." When "mixed with sugar and lime juice and beaten together [on] a plate," the taste was divine.

This passage in *A New Voyage Round the World*, published in 1697, likely presents the first English description of guacamole.

An accomplished navigator, intrepid explorer, naturalist and dedicated foodie, Dampier was instrumental in introducing many of the foods we know today. He also was a pirate and privateer, sampling the local cuisine and observing the flora and fauna in between raids on Spanish ships.

Dampier brought the English-speaking world the words kumquat, chopsticks, barbecue, cashew, soy sauce and tortilla. His writings about breadfruit inspired Britain to transplant the nutritious, easily grown fruit to the West Indies to feed slaves. (It was breadfruit that Captain William Bligh's ship *Bounty* carried when the crew mutinied in 1789.)

Born in Somerset, England, in 1651, Dampier dabbled in logging and sugar-plantation management in Jamaica before joining Captain Bartholomew Sharp's pirate ship in Mexico's Bay of Campeche in 1679, the first of several pirate and privateer adventures that took him from Peru to Virginia. He visited Australia in 1699, decades before Captain Cook, and circumnavigated the globe three times.

While locked in a Spanish prison, he penned *A New Voyage Round the World*, which would make him rich and famous and sparked a travel journal craze that would last centuries—Charles Darwin brought a copy along with him on the *Beagle*.

Combining scientific observations with culinary adventure tales, Dampier wrote of dining on Galápagos tortoises, armadillos, penguins, flamingoes, sea turtles, ostrich eggs, manatee, sea lions, locusts and a prickly pear that turned his urine blood-red "yet found no harm by it." In the Philippines, he tasted mangoes that people cut "in two pieces and pickled them with salt and vinegar, in which they put some cloves of garlic," a dish we now know as mango chutney.

Thanks to the popularity of the book, Dampier avoided scrutiny of his pirating

> *"It is not easy to name another sailor who has supplied such valuable information to the world; [Dampier] had a passion for reporting exactly as he saw it, with a delicate and perfect style."*
>
> **ADMIRAL JAMES BURNEY**

career and was even appointed captain of the British exploration ship HMS *Roebuck* on voyages to Indonesia, Africa and Australia, where his descriptions of Aboriginal tribes as "the miserabilist people in the world" and "differing little from brutes" justified Britain's colonial expansion and genocide.

Dampier never entirely shed his pirate impulses. He was court-martialed for abusing his crew—he marooned those who clashed with him—and he lost the *Roebuck*, his good name and his wealth, dying at age 63, some £2,000 in debt. ⌁

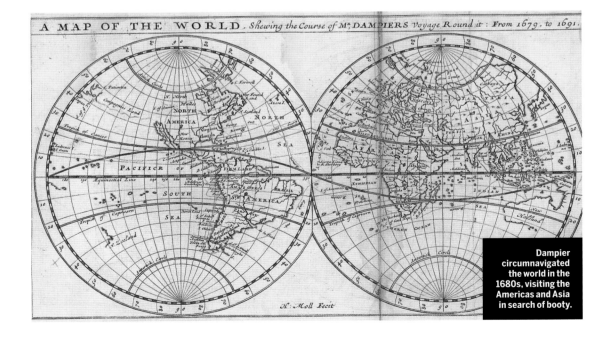

A MAP OF THE WORLD. Shewing the Course of Mr. DAMPIERS Voyage Round it : From 1679. to 1691.

H: Moll Fecit

Dampier circumnavigated the world in the 1680s, visiting the Americas and Asia in search of booty.

William Kidd

He was hanged as a pirate in England, but his spirit still prowls a New York City churchyard

Trinity Church, New York

William Kidd had every intention of becoming a regular parishioner of New York City's Trinity Church. In 1696, the sea captain lent a runner-and-tackle pulley system to construct the church's tall stone steeple; when the church was completed he rented pew No. 4 for himself and his heirs.

As fate would have it, "Captain" Kidd never got to set foot in the church he helped build, nor would he be buried in the churchyard, as he had likely planned. Instead, he was hanged as a pirate in England, his corpse wrapped in iron straps and chains and dangled over the Thames.

Kidd's angry ghost is now said to haunt the little downtown Manhattan church's graveyard in search of the proper burial site that he—and many historians—believe he was wrongfully denied.

Married to a rich widow named Sarah and well connected to a network of powerful political friends in the American colonies, the Scottish-born Kidd had been granted a privateer's license to attack the ships of England's enemy, France.

In January 1698, Kidd scored his biggest prize, raiding the *Quedagh Merchant*, a 400-ton Indian ship carrying gold, silver, satins and silk that was sailing off the western coast of India.

Since the *Quedagh Merchant* was under French protection, Kidd believed his privateering commission gave him the legal right to seize it. Then he found out the captain was an Englishman, which created infinite complications. Kidd tried to get his crew to return the loot, but they refused. Facing a mutiny, the captain kept the booty—and was branded a pirate by England.

While on the run, he sold some loot in the Caribbean and buried the rest on Gardiners Island in Long Island, New York, before being arrested in Boston, where he was lured with a false promise of clemency. After more than a year in solitary confinement, Kidd was sent to England, where he became a pawn in a political battle. His allies deserted him, the French passes from the *Quedagh Merchant*—the keys to his defense—mysteriously got lost before trial, and he was hanged, apparently as a scapegoat to protect his backers.

While the Gardiners Island treasure was dug up, legend has it that Kidd buried more treasure around Long Island. When his ghost isn't seen stomping around the Trinity Church grounds, visitors to the small islands in Long Island Sound have reported seeing Kidd, but refused to say where—for that would reveal the location of the buried loot. ⚓

The pirate is remembered each May in Wildwood, New Jersey, on Captain Kidd Pirate Day, when families don their best buccaneer outfits for a parade down the boardwalk, followed by a treasure hunt on the beach for kids 12 and under.

Sultan Suleiman gave Barbarossa the honorary name Hayreddin, meaning "goodness of the faith."

Barbarossa

*A Muslim sailor became a legend of the
Ottoman Empire fighting the Spanish*

After Spain wiped out the last remnants of Islamic rule in the Iberian Peninsula in 1492, and then sought to conquer the North African coast, besieged Muslim leaders turned to a fighting sailor from the Greek island of Lesbos to help save them.

Born in the 1470s with the name Khidr, the future legend was one of four brothers and two sisters who grew up on the island off the coast of Turkey, now part of Greece but then a bustling Ottoman Empire port and haven for pirates.

As a privateer for various Muslim kingdoms, Khidr sailed oar-powered galleys—more maneuverable in light and shifting winds—in daring and dangerous raids on Spanish and Portuguese ships throughout the Mediterranean.

As successes mounted and his reputation grew, a force commanded by his brother Aruj captured Algiers from the Spanish in 1516. Aruj declared himself sultan, and the brothers joined forces with Spain's primary rival, the Ottoman Empire.

When Aruj was killed in a lengthy battle with the Spanish in 1518, Khidr took Aruj's title of Baba Aruj, or Father Aruj, which their European foes pronounced as Barbarossa, the Italian word for red beard. The newly minted Barbarossa led the Turkish forces, and when he captured Tunis in 1531, he was named the grand admiral of the Ottoman Empire. Informally, he was known as the King of the Sea. After a distinguished naval career that secured the eastern Mediterranean for the Ottomans, Barbarossa retired to write his memoirs in 1545. He died as a hero a year later at about age 67. ⚓

THE TOMB OF BARBAROSSA

In a port on the eastern side of Istanbul, where Barbarossa's fleet once assembled, stands his tomb. For centuries, Ottoman ships setting sail would fire their guns in honor of the commander who came to symbolize Ottoman naval superiority in the Mediterranean. As the empire crumbled, the tradition ended in the 19th century. It dramatically returned in September 2019, when a Turkish naval fleet returning from a massive drill saluted Barbarossa, the guns sounding for the first time in centuries.

L'Olonnais beheaded all but one crewman on a Spanish ship, sending him back with a warning message.

François l'Olonnais

The French privateer found sick pleasure in torture

The most notorious privateer of the late 17th century, François l'Olonnais channeled his overwhelming rages and lust for revenge as a twisted master of torture, cutting out his victims' throats and skinning them alive. Even the most savage cutthroats trembled at the very thought of this sadistic buccaneer.

The source of his depthless anger was the Spanish. Born Jean-David Nau in France around 1630, his family was so poor they sold him into indentured servitude at age 15 to a sugar plantation in the modern-day Dominican Republic, where his Spanish overlords whipped and overworked him. He emerged from nine years of toil and abuse with a burning lifelong hatred for Spain.

Giving himself the more romantic name of l'Olonnais, he secured a privateer commission from the governor of French-controlled Tortuga and unleashed his bloody revenge on Spanish settlements in what is now Central and South America, as well as against Spain's ships throughout the Caribbean.

In all likelihood a psychopath, l'Olonnais tortured prisoners mercilessly to extract the location of treasure. "If the wretch did not instantly answer his questions, he would hack the man to pieces with his cutlass and lick the blood from the blade with his tongue," wrote one chronicler, "wishing it might have been the last Spaniard in the world he had thus killed."

Adept at survival—l'Olonnais once hid under the bloody corpses of his own slaughtered men to avoid capture—he met his end in an appropriately violent and macabre way: After his ship ran aground off the coast of Nicaragua in 1669, he made camp on shore, where natives killed his crew with poisoned arrows and burned l'Olonnais alive before cutting him up and eating him. ⚓

WHEN HE ATE A BEATING HEART

After Spanish soldiers ambushed François l'Olonnais in Honduras in 1667, he fought off his attackers and got away—but not before capturing two soldiers. Using his cutlass, l'Olonnais cut open the chest of one of the men, then "with sacrilegious hands," according to an account, took out his heart and "began to bite and gnaw it with his teeth, like a ravenous wolf." The surviving soldier quickly helped l'Olonnais find a safe escape route.

Black Caesar

*The mysterious and massive pirate made
a failed final stand for his captain*

So little is known about the pirate called Black Caesar that researchers can't agree on whether there were one or two of them. By some accounts, Caesar was an African chief renowned for his "huge size, immense strength and keen intelligence," one writer said, who was captured by slave traders.

When the slave ship was threatened by a hurricane, Caesar and a sailor who had befriended him escaped aboard a longboat loaded with weapons and made their way to the Florida Keys to wait out the storm while the rest of the crew perished. Posing as shipwrecked sailors, they boarded would-be rescue ships, then extracted ammunition and supplies at gunpoint.

After a falling out between the pair—Caesar was said to have killed his partner in a duel over a woman—Caesar led his own pirate raids from under the cover of Florida's mangrove islands, where legend has it he buried as much as $6 million worth of silver bars that have never been found.

By 1718, a seaman by the name of Black Caesar was a top sailor for the famous pirate captain Blackbeard, whose crew was two-thirds Black pirates—escaped and freed slaves—although it's debated whether this was the Black Caesar from Florida or a former slave from North Carolina.

Whoever he was, this Black Caesar battled to the very end, threatening to blow up Blackbeard's ship when it came under attack, before Blackbeard was killed and Black Caesar was captured. Caesar was tried for piracy and executed by hanging in Williamsburg, Virginia. ⚓

HIS LOST CHILDREN

While hiding out on an island in Florida's Biscayne Bay, near present-day Miami, Black Caesar was said to have kept a harem of 100 women kidnapped from passing ships. Legend has it he abandoned the women, their offspring and other prisoners, and that some of the kids survived on shellfish and berries and formed a society of lost children with its own language. Today, superstition has it that their ghosts haunt the tiny islands around Elliott Key and Old Rhodes Key.

Caesar Rock, a small island located north of Key Largo, Florida, is named in his honor.

Stede Bonnet

After a breakdown, the former army major abandoned his family and went rogue

Stede Bonnet retired from the English army with the rank of major and settled down with his wife and three sons as a landed gentleman on a sugar plantation in Barbados that he inherited from his father.

Then one day in 1717, Bonnet snapped. He dumped his wife and kids, purchased a sloop that he christened the *Revenge*, outfitted it with 10 cannons, engaged a crew of 70 and became a pirate captain.

Some believe he was mentally ill; others say that he had simply grown tired of a nagging wife. Whatever the reason, the abrupt career change in his late 20s didn't go smoothly at first for this novice captain. But his experienced crew made up for his nautical ineptitude—the *Revenge* seized a handful of treasure-laden ships—and what he lacked in seamanship skills he made up for in sartorial splendor, earning him the nickname "Gentleman Pirate."

In Honduras, he met up with the infamous pirate Blackbeard, who took one look at the portly, landlubberly Bonnet and decided to forcibly relieve him of his ship, maroon his crew and hold Bonnet himself prisoner aboard Blackbeard's *Queen Anne's Revenge*.

Bonnet managed to escape and reunite with the *Revenge* and his men. He continued pirating for a few months until he was caught, tried and hanged in South Carolina in 1718 at about age 29. His romp as a rogue lasted less than two years. ⚓

Blackbeard easily capture the Revenge

"I implore you to consider me with a Christian and charitable heart, and determine mercifully of me."

STEDE BONNET'S LETTER TO THE GOVERNOR, ASKING FOR CLEMENCY

One account in Bonnet's lifetime claimed "some Discomforts he found in the married state" led to "this Humour of going a-pyrating."

Charles Vane

A fearsome villain, the captain was known for his cruelty and cowardice

CHARLES VANE.

As one of the last pirate captains of his kind, Vane's death is seen as the end of the Golden Age of Piracy.

Although captured and pardoned by King George I, Vane soon returned to his notorious ways.

By all accounts, Charles Vane was a nasty person. Not satisfied with merely raiding and looting a ship, the pirate captain also chose to beat, torture and kill the other sailors. Even other pirates thought he went too far.

After sailing under Bermuda-based English privateer Henry Jennings, Vane went solo in the summer of 1717 and became one of the most feared seafaring villains of the Caribbean.

After he and his sloop the *Lark* were captured, Vane was released in a show of goodwill and accepted one of the pardons being issued to pirates by King George I. But he then promptly returned to piracy, torturing and killing with abandon.

In November 1717, Vane confronted a large frigate by flying his Jolly Roger. The frigate responded with the French naval ensign and blasted Vane's ship into a retreat that his crew—who wanted to stay and fight—saw as an act of cowardice. After voting Vane out as their captain and installing "Calico" Jack Rackham

(see page 110), Vane and a few loyalists were sent away on a small sloop.

Vane returned to piracy until a hurricane stranded him on a deserted island. A would-be rescue backfired when an English ship arrived and he was recognized by an old friend, former pirate Captain Holford, who refused to let him on board. He was picked up by another ship but Holford spotted him on that vessel, too. Vane was arrested, imprisoned for four years and hanged. His body was displayed at Port Royal in Jamaica as a warning. ⚓

"I shan't have you aboard my Ship, unless I carry you a Prisoner; for I shall have you caballing with my Men, knock me on the head, and run away with my Ship."

CAPTAIN HOLFORD TO VANE, IN
A GENERAL HISTORY OF THE PYRATES

Henry Morgan

The pirate captain who inspired a rum spent his time mostly drunk

Morgan was given a state funeral; an amnesty was declared so that pirates and privateers could pay their respects without being arrested.

Morgan destroyed a fleet from the Spanish Armada off the coast of Maracaibo, now Venezuela.

The popular rum Captain Morgan was in fact inspired by a real-life pirate, one Henry Morgan, a Welshman who became a terror of the Caribbean, his men raping and pillaging through Spanish settlements in the 17th century.

Morgan was named second-in-command of buccaneers raiding Dutch settlements in the Caribbean, then in 1662 got his first command of a privateer ship that attacked Santiago de Cuba. He was granted a privateer license by his friend, Jamaica's governor, Thomas Modyford. That gave Morgan—who married his cousin Mary Morgan, the daughter of the island's deputy governor— carte blanche to target Spanish shipping in the region, even though Spain and England were technically at peace.

Modyford justified the move on fears of a Spanish invasion. But while Morgan was supposedly allowed to only conduct raids at sea, he raided Spanish settlements anyway. In 1666, he was made colonel of the Port Royal, Jamaica, militia and elected admiral by his fellow privateers. His most devastating attack was the 1668 invasion of the town of Portobelo, Panama, where his men raped, pillaged and tortured residents.

When Morgan returned to Port Royal, the Admiralty court exonerated him, though he—and Modyford—would run afoul of the government off and on for years over Morgan's continuing raids. Morgan, who was knighted by King Charles II in 1674, died in 1688 at age 53—wealthy and, appropriately, very drunk. ⚓

Thomas Tew

The sea rover amassed a huge fortune by discovering the Pirate Round

A generation of pirates owe their riches to Captain Thomas Tew. A 17th-century privateer believed to have come from Rhode Island, Tew was the first captain to sail what became known as the Pirate Round, a route from the western Atlantic Ocean, around the tip of Africa, and on to the treasure ship-rich waters in and around the Red Sea.

Pirates who followed this course were known as Roundsmen and they included some of history's most famous names, including William Kidd and Henry Every. They would usually return from these hunting grounds along the same route, stopping in Madagascar while awaiting favorable winds to take them back to the Caribbean or American colonies.

While much of Tew's early years remain hazy, he already had privateering experience under his belt when he first appeared in official records in 1691 in Bermuda, where officials granted him a letter of marque to attack French holdings in Africa.

Investors ponied up the funds for Tew's 70-ton, eight-gun sloop, *Amity*, on which the newly licensed privateer and his crew of 46 men set off for Gambia in western Africa. Once away from Bermuda, Tew asked his crew if they wanted to take a vote to abandon the government-backed privateer and turn pirate. They heartily chanted back, "A gold chain or a wooden leg, we'll stand with you!"

To a point, anyway—a quartermaster was also elected to keep Tew in check. Rounding Africa and entering the Red Sea through the Gulf of Aden, the *Amity* encountered a ship from India, which Tew's men seized with little resistance. A search of the hold yielded a staggeringly rich stash of gold, silver, spices, gems and ivory.

When split up among the crew, each man walked away with a share worth more than $3 million in today's money. This single haul made up the bulk of Tew's career earnings, estimated by *Forbes* magazine to be worth nearly $113 million, making him the third-most successful pirate in history.

Tew wanted to sail on and attack more ships, but his crew of new millionaires had no desire to pirate on. With their objections relayed to their elected quartermaster, Tew had no choice but to turn back, stopping only at the pirate stronghold of St. Mary's on Madagascar for water and supplies.

Paying back his investors with a substantial premium, Tew became a leading member of high society in New York, his connections no doubt also helping him secure a pardon for pirating. His friend, the royal governor, granted him a new privateering license against the French. Once again, Tew went rogue. Instead of sailing from New York to Boston, the *Amity* headed back to the Red Sea, joining a pirate convoy headed by Henry Every and his flagship, *Fancy*. In September 1695, the pirates pursued a fleet of Mughal ships, with Tew targeting the *Fateh Muhammed*.

In a bloody battle, the fighters from the Mughal ship managed to repel the *Amity*. Tew was killed by a cannon shot that one historian colorfully described: "A shot carried away the rim of Tew's belly, who held his bowels with his hands for some space." His men surrendered but were freed when Every later seized the *Fateh Muhammed*. ⚓

Tew was said to be one of the founders of the mysterious pirate colony of Libertatia in Madagascar.

"For those who prove worthy, Paradise awaits."

THOMAS TEW

Now owned by the Bermuda National Trust, Dew's old home is open to overnight guests and to day visitors on Wednesday afternoons.

George Dew

His ghost still haunts the Old Rectory, his former home in Bermuda

Harpsichord

Listen carefully in an old bed-and-breakfast in Bermuda for the music of a harpsichord. The player is not living; it's the ghost of a man who was hell on water but who turned around his wicked ways.

George Dew got his sea legs aboard a slave-trading ship, then collaborated with some of the leading pirates of the 17th century. With Francois Groginet and Pierre le Picard, he sacked the town of Guayaquil in Ecuador in 1687. Four years later, he teamed up with "Captain" William Kidd and tangled with French sloops up in the Piscataqua River in what is now New Hampshire. As a privateer, Dew joined Thomas Griffin in outracing famed pirate hunter Christopher Goffe.

Dew's sloop, *Amy*, accompanied Thomas Tew's ship to attack French slave ports in Africa, but a fierce storm cracked the *Amy*'s mast. Dew limped into a southern African port, where the Dutch promptly arrested him for piracy and shipped him off to Holland.

Released for lack of evidence, Dew eventually returned to his wife in Bermuda in 1699, built a pleasant limestone home with multiple chimneys that he called Old Rectory and turned his back on piracy, living out his years as a lawyer and local politician. Perhaps to keep his soul calm, Dew would play his harpsichord. Guests to the still-standing Old Rectory claim they can hear the haunting sounds more than 300 years later. ⚓

CHAPTER 4

WOMEN AT SEA

Men weren't the only ones to roam the waters seeking adventure and booty. As these fearsome females proved, piracy could also be a woman's game, albeit a dangerous one

Ching Shih

The former prostitute commanded tens of thousands of men and ruled a mini-state

S he rose from the humblest of beginnings to lord over a floating kingdom as a pirate leader respected and feared, conquering a male-dominated world with strategic marriages and ruthless brilliance. This pirate queen went by many names in her illustrious life, but history remembers her as Ching Shih, which means simply "Cheng's widow," after her late husband, a pirate named Cheng Yi.

Born in China's Guangdong province in 1775, Ching grew up in the criminal underworld as a young prostitute aboard a floating brothel, known as a "flower boat," where it is believed she honed her skills not just for pleasures of the flesh, but for manipulation, deception and survival.

When Cheng, the commander of the Red Flag pirate ships, asked her to marry him in 1801, she agreed on the condition she get half his plunder and a leadership role. Together they formed a formidable duo in the China Sea, but her husband died a few years later, leaving Ching, as a widowed woman, in a vulnerable position.

In a plan that was bold, audacious and a little kinky, Ching maintained her position by marrying her late husband's adopted son, Cheng Pao, who was his second-in-command—and his lover. The new power couple expanded their fleet of some 1,800 Chinese junks and small boats crewed by

Ching Shih inspired the character of Mistress Ching, played by Takayo Fischer, in the 2007 film *Pirates of the Caribbean: At World's End.*

> *"Deserting or being absent without leave would result in a pirate being paraded through the squadrons with their ears hacked off."*
>
> **CHING SHIH'S CODE OF LAWS**

Some sailors brought their wives and children to live on the Chinese pirate junks.

as many as 70,000 men. They raided Chinese, British and Portuguese ships and extracted taxes from Chinese villages.

As commander of such a large enterprise, Ching became essentially the sovereign of her own independent mini-state, with laws and regulations drafted by her. As the most serious rules were enforced under punishment of flogging and dismemberment, her men "took great care to behave themselves well," one contemporary observer wrote.

Although Ching ruled with an iron fist, she had special rules to protect other women. She forbade the abuse of women and declared that while they could still be taken as slaves and concubines, those not kept for ransom should be sold to the pirates as wives for $40 each. Men who were unfaithful or committed rape were executed. Even consensual sex between unmarried partners called for the man's beheading.

When government forces increased their pressure against Ching Shih and her fellow pirates began to break ranks with her, she negotiated a settlement in 1810 in which she retired from piracy but kept her loot and husband. She lived out her years running a gambling house and brothel in Macau until her death at age 69 in 1844. ⚓

Anne Bonny

Married to another man, she ran away to join her pirate lover, Calico Jack

With her red hair and a fiery temper to match, Anne Bonny could hold her own with the rogues of New Providence Island in the Bahamas, a pirate stronghold where outlaws of the sea could come to get a king's pardon.

The Irish-born Anne was married to a sometime-pirate named James Bonny, who scraped out a living informing on other pirates to the island's governor, leading to many arrests. It may have been Anne's contempt for his activities that drove her into the arms of "Calico" Jack Rackham, another minor pirate. Others say she simply fell in love. Rackham offered Bonny money to divorce Anne, but he refused.

Facing a whipping on adultery charges, Anne ran away with Rackham on the stolen sloop *William* in August 1719. Anne and Mary Read, another woman who was also disguised as a man (for more, see page 112) joined the pirate crew. The ship primarily preyed on fishing boats and small merchant ships around Jamaica.

In October 1720, the *William* was captured by a government-backed pirate hunter while the men were asleep after celebrating a big prize. Only Anne and Mary were awake, and they fought capture "cursing and swearing much" according to court testimony and "ready and willing to do anything."

Tried in Jamaica, the crew was sentenced to hang for piracy in November 1720. "I'm sorry to see you here," Anne told Calico Jack at the gallows, "but if you had fought like a man, you need not have hanged like a dog." Given a reprieve because she was pregnant, Anne gave birth in jail. Her ultimate fate is unknown, and she remains lost to history. ⚓

"Calico" Jack Rackham

Mary Read

*The cross-dressing buccaneer
cursed and fought as well as—
or even better than—the men*

She lived most of her life as a man, but died as a woman. Favoring male clothing from an early age, Mary Read posed as a boy to serve as a "powder monkey," carrying gunpowder to the cannons on a British man-of-war; she reportedly lived as a man while later serving in the army. But when she fell in love with another soldier, she revealed her gender to him—and to her stunned regiment—and the pair married.

It would end unhappily with her husband's death, after which Read returned to living as a man. In 1715, she sailed to the West Indies, where her ship was taken over by pirates, whom she joined either by choice or by force. She fooled them all into thinking she was a man. She developed a reputation for ruthless violence and "cursing and swearing much," one witness said.

Read wound up on the crew of "Calico" Jack Rackham's sloop that also had another crewwoman, Rackham's partner, Anne Bonny, on board. The two women wore men's clothing—trousers, loose tunics and handkerchiefs on their heads—and were armed with pistols and machetes, but they didn't fool at least one person: a woman on a ship they raided. "The Reason of her knowing and believing them to be women then was by the largeness of their Breasts," according to one account. After her capture, Read was sentenced to hang for piracy, but is believed to have died while incarcerated, possibly during childbirth. ⚓

More Fierce Female Pirates

They may not be as well-known as their male counterparts, but these ladies were often just as ferocious

Awilda | *Fairy-Tale Princess*

The daughter of a fifth-century Scandinavian king, Awilda was said to have been locked in a castle tower until a suitor named Alf rescued her. Not knowing he was a Danish prince, Awilda dressed as a man, escaped, and became a pirate. Awilda's story is the stuff of legend in Denmark, right down to the happy ending: According to the tale, a fleet sent by Denmark's king defeated Awilda and took her hostage. As the commander removed his helmet, he revealed himself to be none other than Alf. Smitten, they married on the ship and became the king and queen of Denmark.

Lai Choi San | *Dragon Lady*

She was said to be one of the most powerful Chinese pirates in history, second only to Ching Shih (see page 108, commanding a fleet of 12 junks in the South China Sea during the 1920s and '30s. Lai Choi San inspired the Dragon Lady villain in the *Terry and the Pirates* series in comic strips, radio and TV, which would eventually become a stock role in popular culture. "What a woman she was!" wrote Finnish-born adventurer Aleko Lilius in his 1931 book, *I Sailed With Pirates*. "Her hair jet-black, with jade pins gleaming in the knot at the neck, her earrings and bracelets of the same precious apple-green stone." Lilius claimed to have sailed with her fleet of "fearsome fellow, muscular bare-chested men" in the 1920s. But how much of his account is true is unclear, as Lilius' book is the only source to mention her.

Queen Teuta | *Stood Up to Rome*

When King Agron of Ardiaei died in 231 B.C., his widow, Teuta, took the throne and carried on his campaign to conquer lands and plunder ships along the Adriatic coast. Weary of the attacks, Rome sent two ambassadors to Teuta to call off her forces. She refused, seizing their ship, holding one ambassador captive and killing the other. Rome declared war, sending 200 ships and forcing her to surrender. Rather than face the humiliation of paying tribute to Rome, she stepped down and disappeared into history, though legend says she died by suicide, by jumping off a cliff.

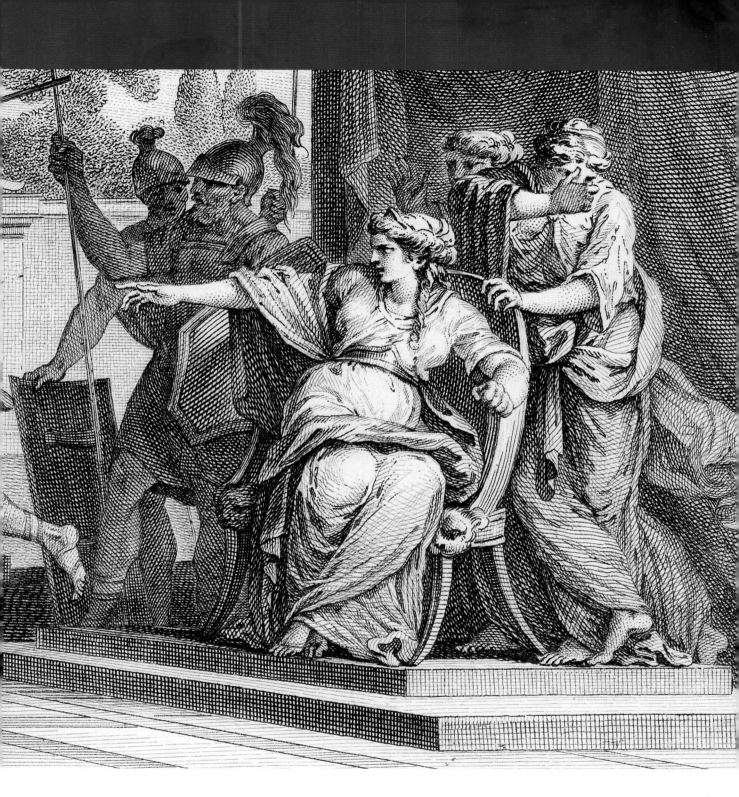

Grace O'Malley | *Queen of the Pirates*

Derided by her foes as "a woman who hath imprudently passed the part of womanhood," and hailed by her supporters as Ireland's 16th-century Queen of the Pirates, Grace O'Malley became chieftain of her clan after her father's death, plundering English ships and defending her land in brash defiance of Queen Elizabeth I during the 1500s. Wrapping herself in a blanket on the deck of her galley as she led her fleet into battle, Grace was a courageous fighter, said to have given birth to a son one day and raiding a Turkish ship the next. One of the few clan leaders to resist Elizabeth, O'Malley repelled an English attack on her base of Rockfleet Castle, forcing a humiliating defeat. But when a newly appointed governor killed her eldest son, locked up her youngest and seized the castle, she changed tactics and sought an audience with the queen, who surprisingly agreed. A wary O'Malley was said to have stashed a dagger for the meeting and refused to bow because she, too, was a queen. Impressed, Elizabeth released her son and returned her castle after O'Malley agreed to help England fight foreign enemies. She died an old, wealthy woman in her castle in 1603.

"The pirates of the Chinese seas make their junks their homes, and carry their wives and children with them on every expedition," Fanny Loviot wrote.

PIRATE KIDS

As a buccaneer's life tends to interfere with stability, most left their wife and kids at home for long periods of time or just abandoned them altogether. Not so for Asian pirates: They turned their junks into floating homes, according to Fanny Loviot, author of 1858's *A Lady's Captivity Among Chinese Pirates in the Chinese Sea.* "The women assist in working the ships, and are chief employed in lading and unlading the merchandise," she wrote. "As for the children, they carry them upon their backs in a kind of bag, till they are able to run alone."

Jeanne de Clisson

"Were it not for [hanging], every cowardly fellow would turn pirate."

ANNE BONNY

Rachel Wall | *New England's Only Woman Pirate*

Born Rachel Schmidt, she fled her home in Pennsylvania at 16 and later married fisherman George Wall, who convinced her to "take bad company," she wrote, "from which I may date my ruin." In 1781, the couple set off from Boston in a stolen ship, raiding vessels and killing dozens of sailors, until George drowned in a storm. Rachel found work as a maid but couldn't resist the outlaw life, stealing "goods and chattles" from ships in Boston Harbor before turning to highway robberies. She was arrested for robbing a 17-year-old girl of her shoes, buckles and bonnet; at her 1789 trial she was sentenced to death. As thousands came out to see her hanged in Boston Common, Rachel, 29, declared the witnesses against her "are certainly mistaken" but "as a dying person I freely forgive them."

Jeanne de Clisson | *The Lioness of Brittany*

Born into nobility in 14th-century Brittany, France, Jeanne de Clisson developed a hatred for the French after King Philip VI ordered the beheading of her husband as an English sympathizer. In 1343, she sold her lands to bankroll her revenge, attacking French ships in the English Channel and lopping the heads off French nobility. After 13 years, she retired to live with her third husband in England before returning to France, where she died in a castle at age 59 in 1359. ⚓

Women Who Married Pirates

Meet the buccaneer wives who loved—and sometimes fought alongside—their men

They rape and pillage and smell bad...not exactly what you'd call ideal husband material. But some women just couldn't resist the bad boys of the sea, according to Daphne Palmer Geanacopoulos, author of 2017's *The Pirate Next Door: The Untold Story of Eighteenth Century Pirates' Wives, Families and Communities*, who discovered that "behind many a pirate was a strong woman on land."

MARY ORMOND, BLACKBEARD'S LAST WIFE

After losing his one true love—his ship *Queen Anne's Revenge*—Edward Teach, aka Blackbeard, applied for a royal pardon. To prove he was going straight this time, he bought a house in North Carolina and, in 1718, married Mary Ormond, who was somewhere between 14 and 16 years old and quite possibly pregnant. She also may have been his 14th wife. The unholy union lasted a few months before Blackbeard went back to his pirating ways and got killed in a sea battle. According to legend, Blackbeard left Mary as a gift to his crew, though her true fate is unknown. She would go down in history as "Poor Mary." Her ghost is said to haunt their old home, which is now a B&B called The Hammock House in Beaufort, North Carolina.

BARONESS CHRISTINA ANNA SKYTTE

The Swedish-born baroness secretly ran a pirating operation with her brother, Gustav, in the 1650s and 1660s, raiding and sinking merchant ships in the Baltic Sea. Gustav was arrested and executed for piracy, but Christina married another partner in the enterprise, Gustaf Drake, and the pair slipped away to Denmark. While on the run, Drake was tried and convicted in absentia and sentenced to relinquish his property. After they returned to Sweden in 1668, Drake secured a pardon, while his wife avoided charges because she was a married woman, and thus considered a minor under the law of the times.

SARAH KIDD

Hands down, Sarah Kidd was historian Geanacopoulos' favorite pirate wife. "I admire her strength and grit," the author told the Library of Congress blog of the wealthy, twice-widowed Englishwoman who wed William Kidd in 1691. "Behind 'Captain' Kidd was a very strong woman who pleaded, cajoled and bribed colonial officials to try to save her husband's life. Their relationship was a real love story"—albeit one that ended tragically, as Kidd was hanged for piracy in England in 1701. In a horrible turn of events, the rope broke the first time and Kidd survived, only to be hanged a second time a few minutes later. His corpse was gibbeted—wrapped in chains—and dangled over London's Thames River for three years as a warning. Sarah Kidd—who had two daughters with the pirate—was also arrested and had her possessions seized, but was released due to lack of evidence. She married a fourth time and purchased a tavern in New York that she ran until her death in 1744.

ANNE DIEU-LE-VEUT

Born in Brittany, France, Anne Dieu-le-Veut arrived in Tortuga in the 1680s as one of France's "Filles de Roi," poor women, often with criminal pasts, who were sent to the colonies to start new lives as wives. Twice widowed, she was said to have challenged buccaneer Laurens de Graaf to a duel for insulting her. He arrived with a sword while Anne packed a pistol. He was so taken with her courage that he married her and they set out on his ship, where she was treated as a mascot who brought good fortune. In 1695, the English captured her and her three children and held them for three years. Upon release, she may have settled in Louisiana, Alabama or Mississippi—the accounts differ—while some believe she resumed a life of piracy with de Graaf. History does record that he died in 1704 and his wife passed six years later, in 1710.

Despite spending long periods at sea, many pirates managed to find love on land.

CHAPTER 5

POP CULTURE PIRATES

Almost everything we think we know about the outlaws of the sea, from walking the plank to rolling their R's, comes not from contemporaneous accounts and history books, but from literature, movies, plays, music and television

Blockbuster

Pirates of the Caribbean resurrected a genre many feared had been buried at sea

"You could see all these worried faces," Johnny Depp says of his improvising on the set. "It gave me fuel to go further."

Jack Sparrow's compass and ring

Although it seems like a no-brainer now, before Disney released *Pirates of the Caribbean: The Curse of the Black Pearl* in 2003, based on its popular amusement-park ride, pirate movies were considered box-office poison. After the disastrous *Cutthroat Island* with Geena Davis and Matthew Modine in 1995—which cost more than $100 million to make and earned only $10 million—failed to regenerate a Hollywood staple that had been dormant for decades, the studios all but blacklisted the genre. Then Johnny Depp changed all that. Led by his zany take on Captain Jack Sparrow, along with cutting-edge special effects, nonstop action and dynamic support from Orlando Bloom, Keira Knightley and Geoffrey Rush, *Black Pearl* grossed $305 million and spawned a five-movie franchise that has reaped $4.5 billion worldwide, with fans hoping for more action to come.

UNUSUAL INSPIRATION

Originally envisioned as the standard swashbuckler who swings in and out of the movie, like Errol Flynn or Douglas Fairbanks, Captain Jack Sparrow morphed into someone far more intriguing once Depp started shaking and baking the character. "I figured this guy has been on the high seas for the majority of his life and therefore has dealt with inescapable heat to the brain," Depp told the website Collider. Disney flipped out, but after Depp threatened to quit, the studio accepted the quirky, wacky vision of Sparrow as an unlikely mash-up of the cartoon character Pepé Le Pew and Rolling

Buccaneers

Stones guitarist Keith Richards. Depp scored an Oscar nomination for his portrayal. (For more on Depp's mashed-up inspiration, see page 128.)

TRADEMARK LOOK

To get the right pirate style, costume designer Penny Rose boiled the wardrobe down to what she called the "basic look": square-cut frock coats with a high pocket and a low pocket, with and without lapels, and with big or small cuffs. She then proceeded to make them look authentically used. "I spend more time on wrecking the clothes, making them look old and worn, than on actually making them in the first place," Rose told the website Business of Cinema. "I have a cheese grater on hand at all times." She worked directly with the stars on their costumes, with Depp wasting no time during his session. "He knows immediately what he likes and what works," she said. And what doesn't work? Changing Jack Sparrow's iconic look from movie to movie. "I was gung ho about giving him some variation—but everyone else, including Johnny, was adamant," Rose shared. "Does Mickey Mouse change his clothes?"

Keith Richards

125

FROM DISNEYLAND RIDE TO MOVIE

While movies from *Dumbo* to *Star Wars* have inspired Disneyland rides, only a few rides have inspired movies. In 2002, just a year before *Black Pearl*, Disney released *The Country Bears*, based on the attraction Country Bear Jamboree. It flopped, grossing only $16.9 million in North America.

Other ride-to-screen efforts have been just as forgettable: *The Haunted Mansion* with Eddie Murphy in 2003, *Mission to Mars* (based on a now-defunct ride) in 2000, and 2015's George Clooney movie *Tomorrowland*, based on an entire section of Disneyland, all underwhelmed. Disney also produced *Jungle Cruise*, starring Dwayne "The Rock" Johnson and Emily Blunt (set for release in the summer of 2021).

MEMORABLE VILLAINS

As the archnemesis of Jack Sparrow in all five films, Geoffrey Rush's Captain Hector Barbossa dies, comes back to life and ends up as a rich and powerful lord of his own pirate fleet. As Rush told The Mouse Castle website, Barbossa is a man with a thick skin—and even thicker whiskers. "I always feel that the hat completes everything," he said. "Once the hat goes on, I enter into the spirit of it and I truly become Barbossa."

If the pirate hat makes Barbossa, then it's the advanced special effects that brought Bill Nighy's Davy Jones to creepy life in 2006's *Dead Man's Chest* and the following year's *At World's End*. The captain of *The Flying Dutchman*, who possesses the souls of dead pirates, sports a beard of tentacles—but while filming, Nighy had nothing but dots on his face and clothing. "You have to remember you're going to have an octopus growing out of your chin and one of your legs is a crab leg and one of your hands is a claw," he told the website chud.com. "So the size of your performance and the tone of your performance is informed by that."

Geoffrey Rush

Ian McShane

Orlando Bloom and Keira Knightley

Penélope Cruz

Bill Nighy, who played Davy Jones, told *Empire* he'd "be there like a shot" if asked to return for a reboot.

Ian McShane channeled the famous real-life pirate Edward Teach, aka Blackbeard, in 2011's *On Stranger Tides*. His own beard, elaborate and uncomfortable, helped him get into character on the sweltering Hawaii set. "The heat, the costume and the makeup all help to concentrate the mind," he told the website movies.ie.

NO DAMSEL IN DISTRESS

Like Jack Sparrow, Keira Knightley's Elizabeth Swann underwent a metamorphosis from the original idea to the character on the screen in *Black Pearl*—from a tightly corseted classic damsel in distress who "sat in a corner, pouted a bit, screamed a lot," pining after Orlando Bloom's Will Turner, to a heroine who got into the action. "As soon as the corset comes off she's liberated, and a bit freer and certainly stronger," Knightley told ScreenSlam— though she's still powered by her love for Turner, which is still "a kind of very girlie thing." ⚓

7 THINGS YOU PROBABLY DIDN'T KNOW ABOUT *PIRATES OF THE CARIBBEAN*

1. Keira Knightley was only 17 when she starred in the first film and was accompanied by her mom to every shooting location.

2. Robert De Niro was offered the role of Jack Sparrow and turned it down because he thought the film would be a flop.

3. During filming of *On Stranger Tides*, Depp spent over $60,000 to buy 500 crew members waterproof jackets to protect them from the cold, wet weather.

4. Johnny Depp improvised a lot of Jack Sparrow's iconic lines and catchphrases, including "savvy."

5. Tom Hiddleston, Tobey Maguire, Ewan McGregor, Jude Law and Heath Ledger were all considered for the role of Will Turner, which eventually ended up going to Orlando Bloom.

6. Depp wore special contact lenses that acted as sunglasses so that he wouldn't squint when looking into the sun.

7. Penélope Cruz was two months pregnant when she began filming *On Stranger Tides*. Once she was showing, her sister, Monica, filled in for the wide-shot scenes.

"Pepé Le Pew was the kind of character who always was able to run between the raindrops. He'd just always make it through."

JOHNNY DEPP, ON HIS CARTOON CHARACTER INSPIRATION

Dead Man's Chest was filmed at such a remote location that Disney reportedly paid for roads to be paved just so the crews could bring in equipment.

Surprising Inspirations for Johnny Depp's Jack Sparrow

Pepé Le Pew

Any resemblances to a rock star or a cartoon skunk are completely intentional

The long straggly hair, the bandanna, the rings, that loopy, rebellious presence, the quippy sense of humor: Captain Jack Sparrow could be the twin brother of Rolling Stones co-founder and guitarist, Keith Richards.

"I started thinking about pirates in the 18th century, how they were the rock 'n' roll stars of that time," Johnny Depp said in an interview with IGN of his thinking process in creating his character for 2003's *Pirates of the Caribbean: The Curse of the Black Pearl*, the movie industry's return to the pirate genre after a string of flops like 1995's money-losing stinker *Cutthroat Island*. "Then, when you think of rock 'n' roll stars, the greatest rock 'n' roll star of all time, the coolest rock 'n' roll star of all time, in my opinion, is Keith Richards. Hands down."

Then Depp took it one big, weird step further. Why not mash up Richards with the randy skunk Pepé Le Pew from the Saturday morning Looney Tunes cartoons Depp remembered as a kid?

"What I loved about Pepé Le Pew was this guy who was absolutely convinced that he's a great ladies' man. And he's a skunk," the actor said. "I always loved a character like that, just blinders, no matter what the actual reality is happening around him. This guy sees only what he wants to see."

Even as Jack Sparrow became an iconic pirate character, Depp told *NME* he was "a little worried at what Keith Richards was gonna think. I didn't fear Pepé Le Pew but I was a little worried about Keith. Because for a good portion of the time I was spending with him, I was sponging as much of him as I possibly could for the character. And when he found out what I'd been doing, it could've gone either way."

Despite worries about how Richards would respond, the rock legend not only loved the portrayal, but himself appeared in two of the films—*At World's End* and *On Stranger Tides*—playing Sparrow's father, Captain Teague. "To be able to then bring him into the fold…and do scenes with him was amazing," Depp admitted. "It's one of those things you know has been seared into your brain and will never leave. It's one of those moments: 'I'm really lucky to be here at this moment, and I'm really lucky that I'm aware that I'm lucky.'" The rock legend enjoyed the experience as well and found parallels between rocking and pirating. "Both," Richards told *Rolling Stone*, "are ways to make a good, dishonest living."

"It's fun and a change, a bizarre other world," Keith Richards said of acting. "If you're used to rock 'n' roll, books and movies are fairly tame."

129

The Original Movie Corsair

Douglas Fairbanks may have been a silent-movie star,
but his film stunts spoke volumes

After slicing and dicing his way through the rollicking silent-movie hits *The Mark of Zorro, The Three Musketeers, Robin Hood* and *The Thief of Bagdad*, Douglas Fairbanks, at age 44, went rogue.

In 1926, the superstar American with the dashing good looks and pencil-thin mustache appeared in what his biographer Jeffrey Vance called a "dazzling new showcase for the actor-producer's favorite production value: himself."

The movie was *The Black Pirate*, an elaborately choreographed silent movie, shot in the then-groundbreaking two-color-tone Technicolor, which featured one of the most famous stunts in movie history: the scene in which Fairbanks stabs his dagger into a ship's sail, then rides the ripping fabric down to the bottom.

It established Fairbanks as *the* movie pirate for all who dared to follow him.

Born Douglas Ullman in Denver in 1883, the actor performed in amateur theater and summer stock through high school before joining a traveling acting troupe as an actor and assistant stage manager. His multiple roles were a preview of his later versatility as actor, writer, producer, director and studio executive.

Moving to New York, he married and welcomed a son, the future actor Douglas Fairbanks Jr., and split his time between acting on Broadway and working in a hardware store before heading to Los Angeles. He signed with Triangle Pictures in Los Angeles in 1915, appearing mostly in comedies.

At a party he met Hollywood's reigning actress, Mary Pickford, and the pair began an affair. (His first marriage ended in divorce.) Their marriage created the first Hollywood power couple, holding court in their famous "Pickfair" estate, and they became part of the founding members of United Artists in 1919, along with Charlie Chaplin and director D.W. Griffith, granting them total control over their movies.

Through the 1920s, Fairbanks specialized in costume adventures that showcased his athleticism, most famously his high-flying moves in *The Black Pirate*. The film is now considered a classic, making two of the American Film Institute's Top 100 lists, for Heroes & Villains and Thrills.

As his health began to suffer from his heavy smoking habit, Fairbanks pulled away from acting—his last silent film was *The Black Mask* in 1929—and his subsequent talkies did poorly. He was divorced from Pickford in 1936, remarried and traveled. He died three years later at age 56. Legend has it that his final words were: "I've never felt better." ⚓

A HOLLYWOOD ECCENTRIC

According to biographer Tracey Goessel, Douglas Fairbanks' second wife, Mary Pickford, constructed a complete exercise center for her fitness-fanatic husband that included a concrete-lined, 6-foot-deep trench that ran parallel to Santa Monica Boulevard in Los Angeles, so that he could jog without being spotted by passing cars. The reason he needed privacy: He ran naked.

MGM studio chief
Louis B. Mayer
famously said,
"Beery's a son of a
bitch. But he's our
son of a bitch."

One-Legged Scene Stealer

Wallace Beery was a character actor who made his mark

A scowling rogue off-screen who scared child actors and embarrassed the studio with his messy personal life, Wallace Beery reigned as Hollywood's leading character actor, commanding top dollar and earning the grudging respect of his bosses.

All this made him the perfect face for pirate adventures, starting in the silent era with 1926's *Old Ironsides*, playing merchant seaman Bos'n, who joins the crew of the USS *Constitution* battling pirates in the Caribbean. For this lavish sea epic, producers spared no expense, burning and sinking a real 1886 ship off California's Catalina Island.

Beery easily transitioned to the sound era starring as the one-legged, parrot-toting Long John Silver in *Treasure Island*, the 1934 take on the classic that also starred Lionel Barrymore and kid star Jackie Cooper (right), who hated and feared Beery.

Behind the scenes, Beery's first marriage, to a 17-year-old Gloria Swanson, ended amid allegations he raped her on their wedding night and forced her to swallow a pill to induce an abortion. His second marriage would also end in divorce, followed by a messy paternity battle over an adopted child. He also reportedly joined other men in a drunken fight outside a Sunset Strip club that left a comic actor dead.

No matter, the studios protected Beery. He was back a year later playing an unsavory character opposite Clark Gable and Jean Harlow in 1935's *China Seas*. ⚓

Treasure Island

A Real-Life

Hollywood's leading pirate, Errol Flynn, earned his rogue chops as a young man

As a young man living in New Guinea and Australia, Errol Flynn claimed to have smuggled guns and diamonds, prospected for gold, trapped birds, managed a coconut plantation, dynamited fish—and engaged in South Seas piracy.

Ready to move on, he asked his biology professor father for money, but his papa promptly refused. "I had to continue to scrap it out on my own," Flynn wrote in his appropriately titled 1959 autobiography, *My Wicked, Wicked Ways*, "find my own directions—get out of New Guinea under my own sail—go where the winds would blow."

Those winds took him to the Australian set of the film *In the Wake of the Bounty*, a hybrid documentary-feature based on the famous 1789 British Navy mutiny. The 1933 movie fizzled at the box office, but the sweet taste of attention from acting convinced the 23-year-old Tasmanian-born Flynn to abandon his life as an arrested adolescent in Australia and pursue an even more debauched existence in Hollywood.

Whether his tales of pirating and the rest were true never seemed to matter to anybody who knew or worked with him. Flynn believed them and, more importantly, exuded their spirit on camera. When the dashing English actor Robert Donat backed out of the big-budget 1935 pirate spectacle *Captain Blood*, citing fears his asthma would hinder the demanding stunts, Warner Bros. saw promise in Flynn, then a relatively unknown contract actor.

Working with another newcomer, 19-year-old Olivia de Havilland (who had her own 50-plus year career, including as Melanie Hamilton in *Gone With the Wind*), Flynn embodied everything moviegoers would want in a pirate. *Captain Blood* earned an Academy Award nomination for Best Picture, the first for a pirate movie, losing, curiously enough, to the Hollywood take on *Mutiny on the Bounty*.

After dazzling audiences as the titular bandit in 1938's *The Adventures of Robin Hood*, Flynn returned to sea in 1940's *The Sea Hawk*, in a Sir Francis Drake–type turn that cemented him as Hollywood's greatest pirate, followed by 1952's *Against All Flags*, his last pirate film.

But his real-life boozing, womanizing, drinking and drug-taking soon caught up with him. With clogged arteries and cirrhosis of the liver, he died of a heart attack in 1959 at the age of 50. ⚓

"He claimed to have indulged in piracy on the South Seas, killed a man in Papua New Guinea, smoked opium in Hong Kong and engaged with the Nazis while smuggling guns."

PAUL WHITINGTON IN
THE IRISH INDEPENDENT

Swashbuckler

Flynn co-starred with Olivia de Havilland in eight films, including 1935's *Captain Blood*.

HIS SON WAS THE TRUE HERO

While Errol Flynn flirted with danger and death on screen, his son (pictured below) did it in real life. A 28-year-old freelance photojournalist, Sean Flynn—who starred in 1962's *The Son of Captain Blood*—was on assignment in the killing fields of Cambodia for *Time* magazine in 1970 when he and another journalist were captured by Communist guerrillas. Neither man's body was ever found, and after spending a fortune searching for Sean, his mother, the French-American actress Lili Damita—who was Errol's first wife—had him declared legally dead in 1984.

Pirate Queen

Fiery actress Maureen O'Hara held her own on land and sea

Her flaming-red hair, green eyes and peachy complexion earned Maureen O'Hara the title of Queen of Technicolor. But it was her strength, spirit and athleticism that made her the Queen of Pirates in some of the most ravishing big-screen swashbucklers.

The Irish-born actress tangles with pirates and gets tossed off a ship in 1942's *The Black Swan* (based on a Rafael Sabatini novel), which she called "everything you could want in a lavish pirate picture: a magnificent ship with thundering cannons, a dashing hero battling menacing villains, sword fights, fabulous costumes."

Though draped in frilly, shoulder-baring dresses, O'Hara easily holds her own against the likes of Tyrone Power (below right) and Anthony Quinn, performing her own stunts and, for later movies, learning to fence. "I was tough. I was tall. I was strong," she once said. "I didn't take any nonsense from anybody."

That included, most of all, Errol Flynn, her co-star in what many consider her best pirate movie, *Against All Flags*. The notoriously hard-drinking screen idol, who once made lewd remarks to her during a World War II bond rally until she threatened to expose him in her speech, was on his best behavior while shooting the 1952 Technicolor classic.

"He came to work prepared, he knew his lines," O'Hara told the *Today* show in 2004. "Only one bad thing he did. By 4:30, 5 o'clock, his drinking would catch up with him. I did all my love scenes to a white chalk mark on a black flag, with the script woman reciting Errol's lines in a monotone." (Flynn would hang up his cutlass after *Against All Flags*, which was his last Hollywood swashbuckler, although he made three more movies in Europe.)

O'Hara carried the film, playing a spirited pirate captain named Prudence "Spitfire" Stevens. The role served as an inspiration for Keira Knightley's Elizabeth Swann in the *Pirates of the Caribbean* films. ⚓

The Black Swan

"She's big, lusty, absolutely marvelous—definitely my kind of woman."

JOHN WAYNE, ABOUT HIS FREQUENT CO-STAR MAUREEN O'HARA

O'Hara did her own stunts, which led to her being cast in other swashbucklers.

The Dancing

Hollywood legend Gene Kelly looked to
a famous movie swashbuckler for inspiration

"I had to dance like a tough kid on the street," Kelly, here with Garland, told *Interview* magazine.

Raider

I n the madcap 1948 musical *The Pirate*, Gene Kelly isn't really a pirate: He's a circus performer pretending to be a pirate to win the heart of Judy Garland, before it all spins out of control when the *real* pirate frames the *fake* pirate so he'll hang.

The sparkling Vincente Minnelli concoction shimmers with romance and music, with songs by Cole Porter, including the showstopper "Be a Clown" that Kelly sings and dances to with the famous tap duo the Nicholas Brothers. MGM executives were wary, however, of what they considered to be some overtly sexual numbers, including at least two tempestuous dance sequences that were cut from the film and never seen again.

Of course, the film features a happily-ever-after ending, but the real appeal of the movie is Kelly's moves. In an otherwise mixed review, *The New York Times* gushed, "Gene Kelly is doing some of the fanciest gymnastic dancing of his career in *The Pirate*—and he's good, very good, indeed." While Kelly only plays a pretend pirate, the inspiration for this signature athletic form of dancing came from one of Hollywood's leading pirate stars, Douglas Fairbanks Sr., whose movements Kelly admired. He also reportedly was influenced by the performances of renowned actor John Barrymore.

But while the plot of the film was light, the atmosphere on the set was considerably tenser, with Garland's erratic behavior from her worsening prescription-drug addiction keeping her away for 99 of the film's 135 shooting days. She and husband Minnelli would divorce in 1951. ⚓

"*It was Douglas Fairbanks Sr. I couldn't believe his grace, his moves, his athleticism.*"

GENE KELLY, ON HIS BIGGEST INFLUENCE

In its 1996 obituary for Kelly, who died at 83, *The Los Angeles Times* called him the "Douglas Fairbanks of dance."

Adventurous Acrobat

Athletic and attractive, Burt Lancaster knew how to stir up action

The Crimson Pirate

A circus acrobat before he became a movie star, Burt Lancaster used his high-flying skills in 1952's *The Crimson Pirate*, a gentle spoof of swashbucklers that pays tribute to Douglas Fairbanks and Errol Flynn. Lancaster sets the winking tone when he tells the audience to "believe what you see," then adds, "No, believe half of what you see," then proceeds to swing from tall sails and tumble from high balconies, joined by his silent sidekick (and former acrobat partner) Nick Cravat.

Lancaster is at his blond and often-shirtless best in this lush Technicolor film as 18th-century pirate Captain Vallo, who seizes a Spanish galleon and heads a band of improbably amiable cutthroats. The rest of the movie is equally as ridiculous, with anachronistic technology (an undersea boat! nitroglycerin bombs!). But it's thrills and chills and romance—the beautiful Eva Bartok (left) plays the love interest, the revolutionary leader's daughter Consuelo—that audiences wanted, and *The Crimson Pirate* delivered. A climactic battle, with Lancaster doing all his own stunts, stands as one of the most exciting action sequences in movie history. ⚓

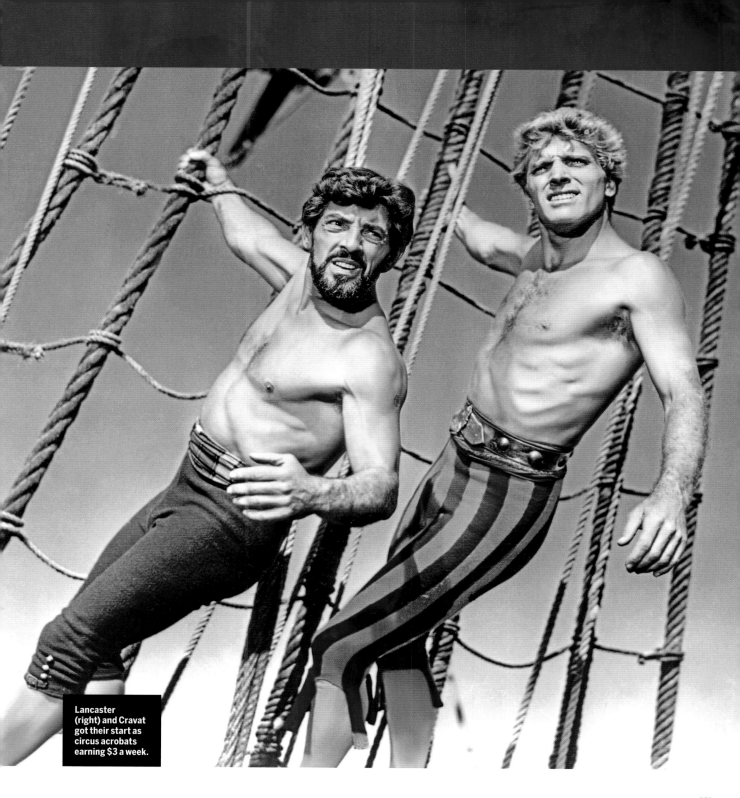

Lancaster
(right) and Cravat
got their start as
circus acrobats
earning $3 a week.

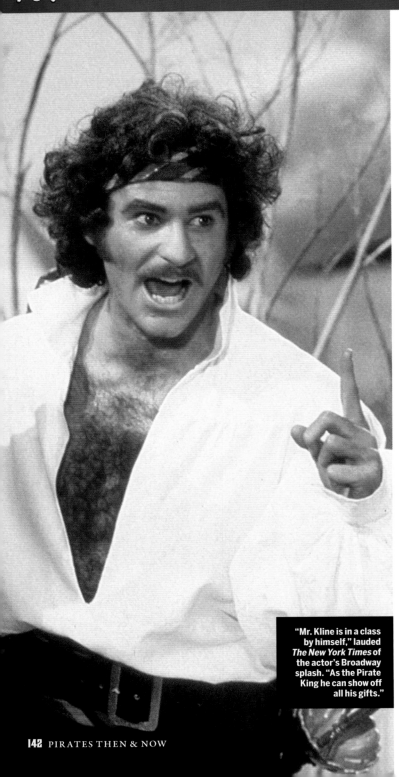

"Mr. Kline is in a class by himself," lauded *The New York Times* of the actor's Broadway splash. "As the Pirate King he can show off all his gifts."

The Singing Pirate

The Pirates of Penzance propelled Kevin Kline to stardom

Gilbert and Sullivan's light opera *The Pirates of Penzance* opened in 1879 to rave reviews. And it still charmed audiences when it was revived on Broadway in 1981—more than a century after its debut—with Kevin Kline in the starring role as the conscience-stricken accidental pirate apprentice. It also featured singer Linda Ronstadt, then at the peak of her rock fame, as the major-general's daughter Mabel.

Kline won a Tony Award for his Errol Flynn–esque turn as the hapless villain Pirate King. "He wants to be bad, but he's really a mush-heart," Kline told *Interview* magazine. "He's honorable, a nobleman gone wrong, gone rough."

Debuting more than 150 years after the Golden Age of Piracy and a follow-up to Gilbert and Sullivan's popular *H.M.S. Pinafore*, the musical makes no claims to historical accuracy. Rather, it pokes fun at operatic conventions, turning the culture of cutthroats into a silly, singing, dancing band of benign romantics.

But while a stage stalwart, the show has sadly not translated as well to the big screen. A movie featuring the original Broadway cast bombed in 1983, undermined by theater owners who were unwilling to screen it in protest of its simultaneous release on paid TV. And another film inspiration, 1982's *The Pirate Movie* with Kristy McNichol and Christopher Atkins, had also fizzled at the box office.

However, the theater version of *The Pirates of Penzance* sails on in local productions and national tours as audiences can't help but agree with the lyrics, "It is a glorious thing, to be a Pirate King!" ⚓

Elwes is firmly against a *Princess Bride* remake: "It would be a pity to damage this one."

Fairy-Tale Hero

Cary Elwes turned heads (and hearts) in The Princess Bride

The Princess Bride

There was never a more dashing and charming pirate than Cary Elwes in 1987's *The Princess Bride*, the handsome swordsman in the black mask. Channeling Errol Flynn at his swashbuckling best, Elwes dishes out the romantic one-liner "As you wish" to his beloved Princess Buttercup, played by Robin Wright (left), then dazzles in an epic battle with Mandy Patinkin's Inigo Montoya. The satirical plot has Elwes' farmhand seeking his fortune so he can marry Buttercup, only to have his ship captured by the notorious Dread Pirate Roberts. In a play on how real-life pirates crafted their own myths, Dread Pirate Roberts is not one man but a title passed on to worthy successors— in this case Elwes' Westley, who becomes the Man in Black out to save Buttercup from Prince Humperdinck and a plot to kill her. Directed by Rob Reiner, the comic fairy tale couldn't find an audience when it opened but later became a cult classic on VHS. "I know that the epitaph on my tombstone will be 'As you wish,'" Elwes told *The Guardian*, "and that's great!" ⚓

"The Princess Bride *is the perfect delivery system for joy.*"

COLLIDER.COM

Playing for Laughs

Pirating isn't always a serious business, as these movies and a comic opera prove

"What did I do to prep?" Hugh Grant mused to the Huffington Post. "Nothing very much, I have to say."

AN ANIMATED ADVENTURE

A band of hapless pirates on a leaky ship has a rollicking adventure with a dodo bird named Polly, a flash card–using chimp named Mr. Bobo, evolutionary scientist Charles Darwin and Queen Victoria. *The Pirates! Band of Misfits* from 2012 would leave a real pirate scratching his beard in befuddlement. This movie shows how far pirate tales have evolved, but it makes perfect sense in this 3D, animated comedy from the creators of *Wallace & Gromit*, with broad comedy for the kids and sly in-jokes for the grown-ups. The Claymation cutthroats are led by the Pirate Captain, voiced by Hugh Grant, who wants nothing more than to win the Pirate of the Year tournament.

A MOTLEY PUPPET CREW

Pirates were at their cuddly cutest in *Muppet Treasure Island*, a musical adventure from the people who created *Sesame Street*, which took the rogues of the seas far from their brutal criminal reality. Based on *Treasure Island*, the 1996 movie takes Kermit, the Great Gonzo and Rizzo the Rat, along with their co-stars—Tim Curry as Long John Silver and Kevin Bishop as Jim Hawkins—to an island in search of treasure. There they find Miss Piggy as queen of the warthogs. As critic Roger Ebert said, the film "will entertain you more or less in proportion to your affection for the Muppets. If you like them, you'll probably like this."

When Tim Curry asked what his billing would be in the film, he was told "first among humans."

Hillary Brooke also played Costello's (center) love interest on *The Abbott and Costello Show*.

STRICTLY SLAPSTICK

Let's get this out of the way now: There's simply no way that "Captain" William Kidd could have joined in an adventure with female pirate Anne Bonny, seeing as Kidd was hanged to death when Anne was only 4 years old. But since the movie's called *Abbott and Costello Meet Captain Kidd*, historical accuracy takes a backseat to comedy. This goofy film from 1952 has the comedy duo of Bud Abbott and Lou Costello tangling with Kidd, played by Charles Laughton—who took the role for only $25,000 because his career had slumped—in a plot involving a love note, a treasure map, Anne (played by Hillary Brooke), a noble lady and a tavern singer. With gags, plus six substandard songs that feel like filler, the movie got bad reviews and earned sympathy for Laughton, who did his best reprising the role he'd played in 1945's Oscar-nominated film *Captain Kidd*. Audiences, particularly kids, loved it.

SCI-FI PIRATES

If somebody tossed every pirate trope, space-movie cliché and fantasy element into a pot, then added some Amazon women, unicorns, Robert Urich, and former football great John Matuszak (below right), this is what they would—and did—end up with. *The Ice Pirates* is a concoction *The New York Times* called "a busy, bewildering, exceedingly jokey science-fiction film that looks like a *Star Wars* spinoff made in an underdeveloped galaxy." This Rotten Tomatoes one-star bomb from 1984 is so bad it made it to badmovies.org, a "website to the detriment of good film." Somehow, producer John Foreman talked his friend Anjelica Huston (below left) into appearing in the movie, which nobody, including the cast and crew, took seriously. As director Stewart Raffill said, "We just put everything we could in it to make a joke and funny and told the story." ⚓

"I had to drink vodka to calm myself down," director Stewart Raffill said after studio heads recut the film's ending.

These Bombs Sank Without a Trace

Some too-terrible pirate tales sent shivers through the industry

HOOK
Over-the-Top Misfire

Hook arrived in theaters in 1991 with great expectations—Steven Spielberg had directed Dustin Hoffman, Robin Williams and a red-hot Julia Roberts a year after *Pretty Woman* made her a star. "All the hype that this movie has gotten," sighed Hoffman to *The Los Angeles Times* of the continuation of

Dustin Hoffman

the story of *Peter Pan*, "is very scary."

He had reason to worry. After reports of cost overruns and star egos—Roberts (as Tinkerbell) and Hoffman (as Captain Hook) were said to be difficult to work with—*Hook* tanked at the box office, becoming the latest pirate film to convince Hollywood that audiences didn't want pirate movies anymore.

Some of the blame went to Hoffman, whose cartoonishly weird characterization left critics and audiences cold. But the verdict was the entire *Peter Pan* sequel not only failed, but failed to justify its existence. As Roger Ebert said in his review, "The failure in *Hook* is its inability to reimagine the material, to find something new, fresh or urgent to do with the *Peter Pan* myth." Even Spielberg was disappointed, saying, "I still don't like that movie. I'm hoping some day I'll see it again and perhaps like some of it."

PAN
Blackbeard Bottoms Out
The 2015 fantasy *Pan* is an alternative origin story for Peter Pan and Captain Hook, starring Hugh Jackman as villainous Blackbeard and Garrett Hedlund as a young Hook, with newcomer Levi Miller as Peter Pan. Jackman—on whom *Pirates of the Caribbean*'s Jack Sparrow had originally been modeled, before Johnny Depp took the role—shaved his head for the film and sang two songs,

Nirvana's "Smells Like Teen Spirit" and The Ramones' "Blitzkrieg Bop." But even his *X-Men* star power couldn't save the movie, which bombed at the box office.

CUTTHROAT ISLAND
The Biggest Pirate Flop of All
Beset by production problems and hammered by critics, *Cutthroat Island* was the acting equivalent of walking the plank. Star Matthew Modine recalled to *Entertainment Weekly* that after a morning of reading the reviews, "I wanted to hang myself in the bathroom." Indeed, Modine admitted that it "kind of damaged my career," he and co-star Geena Davis—a "seriously mismatched romantic duo," according to *Variety*—needed time to recover, though both now have thriving careers and interests. The film is listed in *Guinness World Records* as the biggest box-office bomb of all time—$10 million in ticket sales on a budget of more than $100 million. ⚓

Hugh Jackman

Matthew Modine and Geena Davis

DID THEY REALLY SAY

Arrr and Avast Ye Mateys?

*Most of what we think we know about pirate speech
actually comes from an actor in a 1950s Disney movie*

Since audio recordings didn't exist and pirates rarely wrote down their day-to-day speech, "There isn't much in the way of scientific evidence in regard to pirate speech," historian Colin Woodard told *National Geographic* magazine.

So what little that can be said about how pirates spoke can only be best guesses. Since they were sailors, it's safe to assume that they used nautical jargon, including "avast" and perhaps "matey"— but "shiver me timbers" comes directly from the imagination of writer Robert Louis Stevenson in *Treasure Island*. (For more, see page 153.)

Many pirates likely did speak in a thick English accent, as so many of them came from that country and its numerous colonial outposts, but certainly not all; obviously, a French, Spanish, African or Chinese pirate wouldn't sound like one from the English-speaking towns of Plymouth or Boston.

In reality, most of what we think we know about pirate speech comes from the big screen. The first movie in which pirates said "Arrr" was 1934's *Treasure Island*, starring Lionel Barrymore and Wallace Beery. But the true godfather of pirate speech was British actor Robert Newton, who played Long John Silver in the popular 1950 Disney version of *Treasure Island*, as well as in the 1954 Australian film by the same name, and who also played Blackbeard in 1952's *Blackbeard, the Pirate*. Newton used an exaggerated form of his native West Country dialect to roll his R's ("Arrr" means "Yes" in the West Country). So influential were Newton's performances, says historian Woodard, that "Newton-esque pirates were everywhere, from Captain Hook to Captain McCallister of the *Simpsons* series." ⚓

Lionel Barrymore

Robert Newton

WHO CAME UP WITH TALK LIKE A PIRATE DAY?

Blame it on a racquetball boo-boo. When Mark Summers and John Baur of Albany, Oregon, were playing one day, a wayward ball smacked one of them in the knee, prompting him to say, "Arrr!"…and a new holiday was born. First an in-joke between the two friends, the holiday took off when Summers sent a letter about the idea to humor columnist Dave Barry (right) in 2002. Barry promoted the idea and it went viral. Now, each year on Sept. 19, everyone around the world is encouraged to talk like a pirate.

The Books That Started It All

While countless swashbuckling tomes have been written about pirates, these three are the ones that launched the genre

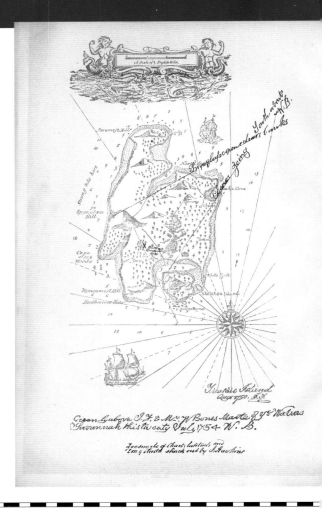

FACT OR FICTION, OR A LITTLE OF BOTH?

Blackbeard was dead only six years when one Captain Charles Johnson published *A General History of the Robberies and Murders of the Most Notorious Pyrates*, the single most influential book about pirates. As a near-contemporaneous account of the lives of the most famous cutthroats of the Golden Age of Piracy, from Bartholomew "Black Bart" Roberts to "Captain" William Kidd, the 1724 book carried considerable weight and is quoted to this day in every buccaneer history. It introduced such pirate clichés as the flying of the Jolly Roger,

and influenced authors Robert Louis Stevenson (*Treasure Island*) and J.M. Barrie (*Peter Pan*). But can it be trusted? With the sources of much of the material impossible to identify, Johnson is presumed to have heavily fictionalized—and romanticized—his biographies. That is...if Johnson wrote the book at all. There is no historical proof that Captain Johnson ever existed, and the book is likely written under a pseudonym—not uncommon for the times. But who was he? One of the most compelling and intriguing arguments is that *Pyrates* was actually written by Daniel

Long John Silver has been played on TV and in films by actors including Charlton Heston, Orson Welles and Eddie Izzard. *Treasure Island* (left) inspired generations of writers.

Defoe, best known for the 1719 novel *Robinson Crusoe*, about a castaway who spends 28 years on a deserted tropical island near Trinidad.

A TALE OF TREASURE MAPS, ONE-LEGGED PIRATES AND PARROTS

When people think of pirates, they're really picturing the colorful characters from *Treasure Island*. Stevenson's 1883 adventure story introduced such staples as the one-legged pirate with a parrot on his shoulder, a treasure map with 'X' marking the spot, rum as the rogues'

drink, and the phrase "Shiver me timbers" and other nautical slang.

The Scottish-born novelist wove these inventions as well as using references to real-life pirates including Blackbeard, Black Bart and Captain Kidd, much of it probably taken from accounts in *Pyrates*, with slightly fictionalized versions of a real governor of Jamaica, an actual tavern called The Admiral Benbow Inn, and the famous 18th-century temperance figure Joseph Livesey.

The result was the single most influential pirate work in history, inspiring other writers, including

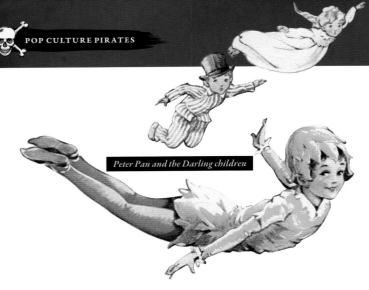

Peter Pan and the Darling children

"Being bashed around in battle…had done nothing good for his brains," Christina Henry wrote in *Lost Boy: The True Story of Captain Hook*.

Peter Pan's Barrie, and countless movies, television shows and plays. And it all began on a cold rainy day in Scotland, when Stevenson's stepson Lloyd Osborne begged the then-writer of travelogues and essays to "write something interesting."

Inspired by drawings of fanciful island maps that the author and young Lloyd had drawn together, along with his recent adventures while living in America, Stevenson set out to create "a story for boys; no need of psychology or fine writing." The yarn of buccaneers and buried gold that told the story of innkeeper's son Jim Hawkins being taken hostage by pirates became *Treasure Island*, originally serialized in a children's magazine called *Young Folks* from 1881 to 1882 under the pseudonym Captain George North. It was published as a book in 1883.

Treasure Island captivated readers with its exciting plot, exotic locations and fanciful figures, led by the cunning cutthroat Long John Silver, who was inspired by a real man (not a pirate): Stevenson's friend, the writer and editor William Henley, "a jovial, astoundingly clever man," wrote Stevenson, "with a laugh that rolled like music."

It was the fact that Henley possessed this spirit despite a disability that had him using a crutch that stirred Stevenson's imagination. "I will now make a confession," the author wrote to Henley. "It was the sight of your maimed strength and masterfulness that begot Long John Silver." Henley's left leg had been amputated below the

knee during a bout with tuberculosis. "The idea of the maimed man, ruling and dreaded by the sound, was entirely taken from you."

Together with his subsequent novels, *Strange Case of Dr. Jekyll and Mr. Hyde* and *Kidnapped*, both in 1886, Stevenson became a celebrity in his own time. But by the 20th century, he had fallen out of favor, relegated as a second-class genre writer, the author of mere stories for boys, excluded from major literary anthologies. Yet as his books and many adaptations on stage and screen continue to charm audiences (see page 158 for more), Stevenson made something of a literary comeback and is now thought by many to be Scotland's greatest writer.

"His eyes were the blue of the forget-me-not, and of a profound melancholy, save when he was plunging his hook into you, at which time two red spots appeared in them."

J.M. BARRIE'S DESCRIPTION OF CAPTAIN HOOK IN *PETER PAN*

PETER PAN'S FICTIONAL BUT FRIGHTENINGLY REAL CAPTAIN

It is from *Peter Pan* that many of our perceptions, and misconceptions, of pirates are born. Take one of the most famous pirate images: As historian David Cordingly writes in *Under the Black Flag*, "Most people assume that pirates made victims walk the plank because that is the fate which Captain Hook was planning for the Lost Boys."

That actual pirates tended to dispense with their victims simply by stabbing them and tossing them overboard does nothing to diminish the power of the *Peter Pan* stories and their villain, Captain James Hook, perhaps the most famous (fictional) pirate of all time. (For more, see page 156.)

Hook—who debuted in Barrie's 1904 stage play, *Peter Pan, or The Boy Who Wouldn't Grow Up*, and has made countless encores in movies, TV shows, plays and other Barrie books—is, of course, named after the prosthetic that replaces the hand that Peter cut off and tossed to the crocodiles. This, along with the peg legged pirate from *Treasure Island*, stands as the prototypical pirate accessory.

For all of Hook's popularity, the captain didn't actually appear in Barrie's early drafts. The author added him later in a small part to distract audiences from scenery changes, then expanded the role to appeal to children's fascination with pirates, stirred by Barrie's friend and fellow Scot Stevenson in *Treasure Island*.

Originally from the upper class, educated at Oxford, dressed like French nobility, Hook was Blackbeard's bosun, Barrie wrote, and "the only man of whom Barbecue was afraid" (Barbecue being both the alias of Long John Silver in *Treasure Island*, and the inspiration for the word buccaneer). He now captains the *Jolly Roger*'s motley crew of comic-relief characters, like clumsy Mr. Snee.

Barrie describes Hook as "cadaverous and black-a-vised, his hair dressed in long curls which look like black candles about to melt." Hook's real name is never mentioned, for doing so, Barrie wrote, "would even at this date set the country in a blaze." He was afraid of only two things: seeing his strange-colored blood and the crocs who ate his hand. Much of the plot of the play and Barrie's 1911 novel version, *Peter and Wendy*, revolved around Hook's quest for revenge. "I've waited long to shake his hand with this," he says looking at his iron hook. "Oh, I'll tear him!" In the 1953 animated feature *Peter Pan*, Disney softened Hook into a temper tantrum–throwing comic villain to avoid scaring young children; it also enacted other changes, like making Pan older, and keeping him alive at the end of the movie.

But Hook maintains his dark grip. Lester D. Friedman's *Second Star to the Right: Peter Pan in the Popular Imagination* sees Hook as a metaphor for death, which, combined with the crocodiles as representing the inevitable passage of time, two of Pan's greatest fears—and arguably those of most children—make the fairy-tale character of Hook as real as any pirate from history. ⚓

WHEN *PIRATES OF THE CARIBBEAN* MET *GAME OF THRONES*

The TV series *Black Sails*, which debuted in 2014 and ran for four seasons, was written as a down-and-dirty prequel to *Treasure Island*. The Starz series, set roughly 20 years before Robert Louis Stevenson's tale, told the story of Captain Flint (Toby Stephens), who takes on a new crew member named John Silver (Luke Arnold) as they search for a Spanish treasure galleon in the Bahamas. Described by *Entertainment Weekly* as "not even a guilty pleasure" but "arrrrrrr-estingly good," the series featured plenty of blood and sex, which led to comparisons to HBO's *Game of Thrones*. Several real-life pirates were fictionalized in the series, including Blackbeard, Anne Bonny and Charles Vane.

Christopher Walken in Peter Pan Live! *(2014)*

Corey Burton voiced Hook in Jake and the Never Land Pirates *(2011–2016)*

PETER PAN'S WICKED CAPTAIN HOOK

Since the debut of the most famous pirate who never existed, Captain Hook has enticed a parade of actors eager to play the one-handed character, and in one case, without his legendary prosthetic. In the 1953 animated classic *Peter Pan*, Disney softened Hook, who was voiced by Hans Conried, into a comic villain to avoid scaring young audiences—a portrayal that would set the Hook standard. A string of actors have since experimented with different interpretations, with varying degrees of success.

Take Dustin Hoffman. His vision of Hook as an over-the-top cartoon pirate with weird shades of William F. Buckley, in Steven Spielberg's all-star 1991 *Hook*, turned off critics, audiences and even Spielberg, who endured a rare flop.

Tim Curry found more success with the role, picking up a Daytime Emmy Award for his turn as Hook in the Fox animated series *Peter Pan and the Pirates*. In 2014, Christopher Walken was so eager to play Hook that he did it on live television in NBC's *Peter Pan Live!* "There's something about him that's sort of sweet," Walken told *The Hollywood Reporter*. "Peter Pan chopped his hand off and fed it to a crocodile, and now he's got a crocodile following him."

A year later, Garrett Hedlund played a pre-hook Hook in the origin story *Pan* that keeps both of his hands intact and only hints at the villain he'll become. "Hook is still very selfish and has his best intentions at hand, his priorities first and foremost," Hedlund told Collider. "But he's a little maniacal. He's crazy in this one, which is fun."

No matter how Hook is interpreted, it is a testament to Barrie's imagination that virtually everything people think they know about pirates comes from Hook, even if it's untrue.

> *"One thing about pirates, they don't care about what anyone thinks, Captain Hook most of all. He really doesn't care what anyone thinks of him."*
>
> JASON ISAACS

Hans Conried voiced the captain in Peter Pan *(1953)*

Jason Isaacs in Peter Pan *(2003)*

Garrett Hedlund in Pan *(2015)*

Rhys Ifans in the miniseries Neverland *(2011)*

Colin O'Donoghue in ABC's Once Upon a Time *(2011–2018)*

Dustin Hoffman in Hook *(1991)*

TREASURE ISLAND'S LEGENDARY LONG JOHN SILVER

The pirate captain of literature gets his most famous lines from the movies.

The iconic cutthroat introduced in *Treasure Island* in 1883, Long John Silver has been refined over the decades by Hollywood. Described as tall and strong despite the peg prosthetic, the result of losing his leg in battle while serving in the British Navy, Silver has proven to be catnip for Hollywood's leading actors eager to strap on the peg leg.

Charles Ogle was the first to portray Silver, in a 1920 silent film, and Wallace Beery was the first to give him a voice in a 1934 MGM talkie. Orson Welles, Tim Curry (co-starring with singing Muppets) and Jack Palance, in his last film role in 1999, all put their spin on the captain.

Anthony Quinn was an outer-space version of Silver in a 1987 TV miniseries, while Charlton Heston embodied a darker shade of Silver in a 1990 TV movie. Woody Harrelson's Tobias Beckett in *Solo: A Star Wars Story* was said to be inspired by Silver, and Luke Arnold played Silver as a young man in the TV series *Black Sails*, set two decades before *Treasure Island*. Eddie Izzard tackled the role in a 2012 miniseries.

The most famous film Long John Silver is British actor Robert Newton, who played him multiple times (as well as Blackbeard) in movies and television. His best-known turns are the 1950 Disney film *Treasure Island* and the 1954 sequel *Long John Silver*, in which he delivers those talk-like-a-pirate-day "arrr"s and "matey"s—none of which are in the book.

Tim Curry in Muppet Treasure Island *(1996)*

Luke Arnold in Black Sails *(2014–2017)*

Charlton Heston in
Treasure Island *(1990)*

Wallace Beery in
Treasure Island *(1934)*

Orson Welles in
Treasure Island *(1972)*

Robert Newton in
Treasure Island *(1950)*

Eddie Izzard in
Treasure Island *(2012)*

CHAPTER 6

FASCINATING STORIES

Off the beaten historical path are lesser-known tales of Julius Caesar's comically brash brush with pirates, women who were kidnapped by pirates—or married their ghosts—and apparitions cruising the afterlife

The Biggest Buccaneer Blunder of All Time

When sea-faring rogues kidnapped the future Roman emperor, he quickly turned the tables on them

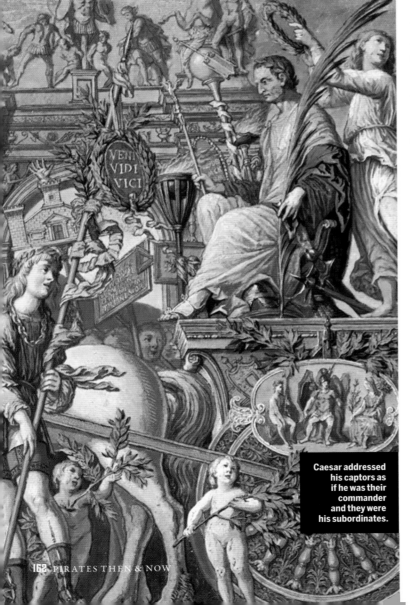

Caesar addressed his captors as if he was their commander and they were his subordinates.

E t tu, matey? One little-known fact about the great Roman emperor Julius Caesar is that as a younger man he was kidnapped and briefly held by pirates. How he wriggled out of the ordeal was pure Caesar.

In the first century B.C., the Mediterranean Sea was swarming with buccaneers who were very much like the swashbucklers of 17 centuries later. Raiding ships and settlements, these cutthroats of the ancient world became an embarrassment to the Romans, who, despite their supreme power, were seemingly incapable of stopping the pillaging.

In 75 B.C., a 25-year-old Caesar, then a Roman nobleman, was sailing through the Aegean Sea on his way to the Greek island of Rhodes to study public speaking when his ship was raided by Cilicians, the most notorious pirates of all, who hailed from what is now Turkey.

They held him captive on their island hideout, but quickly found out they had snatched the wrong Roman. When the pirates demanded a ransom of 20 talents of silver (worth about $600,000 today), "Caesar burst out laughing," the Greek author Plutarch wrote. "They did not know, he said, whom it was that they had captured, and he volunteered to pay 50." The pirates naturally agreed.

Although he was accompanied by only two servants and a friend and greatly outnumbered, Caesar showed no fear. Instead, he subjected the

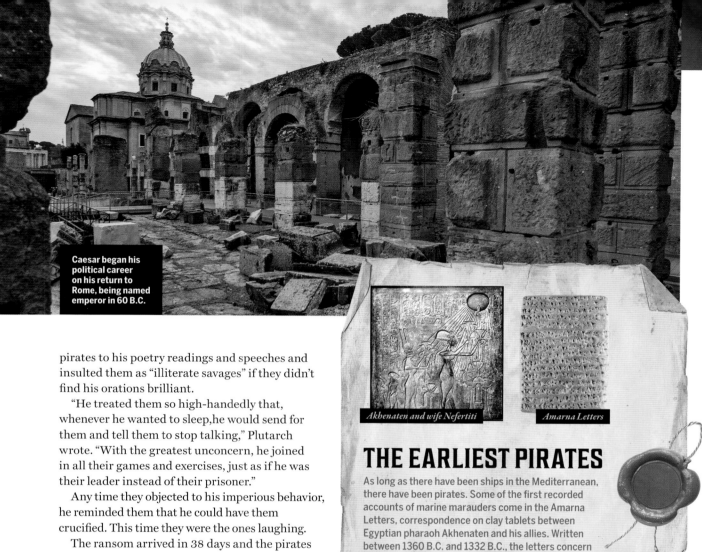

pirates to his poetry readings and speeches and insulted them as "illiterate savages" if they didn't find his orations brilliant.

"He treated them so high-handedly that, whenever he wanted to sleep, he would send for them and tell them to stop talking," Plutarch wrote. "With the greatest unconcern, he joined in all their games and exercises, just as if he was their leader instead of their prisoner."

Any time they objected to his imperious behavior, he reminded them that he could have them crucified. This time they were the ones laughing.

The ransom arrived in 38 days and the pirates sprung him, only to encounter Caesar again—now with a naval force he'd quickly raised. The Cilicians had never bothered to leave the island, so Caesar took back the 50-talent ransom, rounded up the pirates and tossed them in a prison in the Greek coastal city of Pergamon.

When the local official didn't follow Caesar's order to execute the culprits—wanting instead to sell them as slaves and pocket the proceeds—Caesar snatched the pirates from the prison himself and "crucified the lot of them," Plutarch wrote, "just as he had often told them he would do when he was on the island and they imagined that he was joking." ⚓

Akhenaten and wife Nefertiti

Amarna Letters

THE EARLIEST PIRATES

As long as there have been ships in the Mediterranean, there have been pirates. Some of the first recorded accounts of marine marauders come in the Amarna Letters, correspondence on clay tablets between Egyptian pharaoh Akhenaten and his allies. Written between 1360 B.C. and 1332 B.C., the letters concern two groups of pirates who were running rampant. An allied king denies being linked to the outlaws and vows to punish any of his people if they turn to piracy.

"If they failed to admire his work, he would call them to their faces illiterate savages, and would often laughingly threaten to have them all hanged."

PLUTARCH'S *LIFE OF JULIUS CAESAR*

163

The Man Who Inspired Robinson Crusoe

Scottish seaman Alexander Selkirk's four-yearlong castaway adventure turned him into a celebrity—and the star of a classic novel

If ever a man was a perfect candidate to live for years apart from the rest of society, it was Alexander Selkirk. Growing up in a Scottish fishing village in the late 1600s and early 1700s, Selkirk was often drunk and quick to anger and brawl with anybody, including members of his own family.

After one particularly nasty fight in which he assaulted not only his father, but his two brothers and even one of his brother's wives, Selkirk sought refuge from his inner demons at sea, signing on with the *Cinque Ports*, one of two ships under the command of English privateer William Dampier.

The voyage around the tip of South America yielded Spanish plunder—but low food supplies, the deteriorating ship and raging disease brought the crew to the brink of mutiny against the arrogant 21-year-old captain, Thomas Stradling.

After a stop to resupply in the fall of 1704 on one of the uninhabited Juan Fernández Islands off the coast of Chile, Selkirk refused to leave, saying the leaky, wormhole-ridden ship couldn't survive the high seas or another pirate battle.

A livid Stradling left Selkirk on the island with tobacco, cheese, jam, some clothes, a hatchet, knife, a boiling pot, a pistol and musket, gunpowder, a Bible and rum. Selkirk eventually begged to be taken back on board but Stradling sailed away to make an example of him.

For the next four years and four months, Selkirk lived as a castaway, building shelter out of pepper trees, forging a knife out of barrel hoops that washed ashore, setting fires with his musket flints and dining on the island's bountiful food sources: crayfish, goat, turnips, cabbage tree leaves and fish.

Fighting loneliness and despair, he sang psalms and read from the Bible as he kept watch atop a tall cliff for friendly ships—any Spanish crew would likely torture or imprison him or sell him into slavery due to his pirate past. But then on Feb. 2, 1709, he spotted the *Duke* on the horizon.

The crew of the *Duke*, captained by English privateer Woodes Rogers, rescued the heavily bearded, goatskin-wearing Selkirk, who could barely form sentences because he'd gone so long without speaking to anyone. Fortunately, the *Duke*'s navigator was none other than William Dampier, who recognized Selkirk and gave him the news: the *Cinque Ports* had sunk off Colombia, with Stradling and a few other survivors sent to Spanish prisons.

Returning to England after two more long but profitable years of privateering, Selkirk became a celebrity when his story appeared in books by Rogers and Irish author Richard Steele, who in turn inspired British author and political activist Daniel Defoe to write *The Life and Strange Surprizing Adventures of Robinson Crusoe*. Published in 1719, the book became an international bestseller and endures as a classic.

But Selkirk struggled to adjust to life back in civilization, yearning for the simple happiness and peace he had enjoyed on the island, "his Life one continual Feast, and his Being much more joyful than it had before been irksome," as Steele described it.

Defoe, who probably never met Selkirk, moved the castaway's island from the Pacific to the Caribbean for his novel.

In 1720, Selkirk returned to the sea at age 44 as a master's mate on the pirate-hunting Navy ship HMS *Weymouth*. But the voyage to Africa was a cursed one, with disease—either yellow fever or typhoid—wiping out the crew. He died of fever on Dec. 13, 1721, his body tossed into the sea. ⚓

Ghost Ships

On these vessels, you got first class, second class and dead class

With the pump inoperative and the hull full of barrels, Briggs couldn't determine if the ship was in imminent danger of sinking.

Mysteriously abandoned, these ships have been spotted drifting without captain or crew or any connection to the real world. Some of these ghost ships are the stuff of seafaring myth, but others are well-documented, although difficult to explain.

MARY CELESTE

Found adrift in the Atlantic Ocean eight days after leaving New York in 1872 bound for Italy, the 282-ton *Mary Celeste* was missing her lifeboat, the log book and, most importantly, all 11 on board, including Captain Benjamin S. Briggs, his wife, their 2-year-old daughter and eight crew. Theories of why the experienced captain would have abandoned ship include mutinous sailors drunk off the cargo of 1,700 barrels of alcohol, a pirate attack, killer waterspouts, an aggressive giant octopus, sea monsters and space aliens. A more likely scenario, presented in the 2007 documentary *The True Story of the Mary Celeste*, is the captain—worried about a broken chronometer and a faulty pump —abandoned ship shortly after sighting the Azores island of Santa Maria. The *Mary Celeste* essentially sailed herself for hundreds of miles, while the lifeboat never made it to land.

FLYING DUTCHMAN

A ghost ship that really gets around, the *Flying Dutchman* hearkens back to the Dutch East India Company during Holland's 17th-century reign as a great maritime power. The first printed reference to the ship, in 1790, describes weather-beaten sailors spotting the *Flying Dutchman*, the legendary storm-tossed ship that sought safe harbor from the Cape of Good Hope "but could not get a pilot to conduct her and was lost and that ever since in very bad weather her vision appears." Since then, the *Dutchman* has appeared in books, paintings, an opera, and the nightmares of terrified mariners who consider the ship an apparition of doom. Not confined to oceans, the *Dutchman* has been sighted gliding under the moonlight on New York's Hudson River off the shores of Sleepy Hollow.

In 1933, the crew of another ship tried to pull the *Baychimo* free of an ice pack, but it wouldn't budge. They took some items from the ship that ended up at an Alaska museum. The artifacts sat in a drawer for decades until being rediscovered in 2015.

SS BAYCHIMO

When this Swedish cargo ship got trapped in ice off the coast of Alaska in 1931, the crew abandoned ship and made their way over a half-mile of ice to the town of Barrow for shelter. When they returned two days later, the SS *Baychimo* had snapped out of the ice, drifted away, then got stuck again. Although she was presumed sunk by a powerful blizzard, the *Baychimo* would appear countless times over the next 38 years, drifting off the northwestern coast of Alaska. Due to foul weather and lack of equipment, nobody was able to salvage her. The last time anyone saw the *Baychimo* was in 1969.

LADY LOVIBOND

According to legend, this schooner was driven into the rocks off the coast of southeast England in 1748 by the ship's first mate, who was jealous that his lady love married the captain instead of him. All on board—including the newlyweds—were said to have perished—and every 50 years since then, the ship reportedly appears as an apparition.

"The Bermuda Triangle is one of only two places on Earth where true north and magnetic north line up, which could make compass readings dicey."

NATIONAL GEOGRAPHIC

OCTAVIUS

In October 1775, a whaling ship was said to have spotted the *Octavius*, a three-masted schooner, adrift west of Greenland. Below deck were all 28 crew members, frozen solid and perfectly preserved. The captain was found frozen in his cabin, still at his table holding a pen. Next to him were the frozen bodies of a woman and a boy under a blanket. Legend has it the captain had gambled on taking a theoretical shortcut known as the Northwest Passage but got stuck in sea ice and the icy corpses had remained in place ever since. ⚓

THE BERMUDA TRIANGLE

Ever since Christopher Columbus' compass went haywire while sailing through the area, this infamous swath of the Atlantic Ocean—bounded by Miami, Bermuda and Puerto Rico—has an eerie reputation for swallowing ships and planes whole, often in good weather, without so much as an SOS call. These mysteries include the loss of a Navy cargo ship, the USS *Cyclops*, in 1918, and the disappearance of five Navy bombers during World War II. While many blame ghosts or aliens, scientists insist that no more craft are lost, proportionally speaking, in this area of busy shipping lanes and flight paths than anywhere else in the world.

Bermuda Triangle

Modern-Day Piracy, Torture and Death

Judith Tebbutt was kidnapped and terrorized by Somali marauders

The moment Judith Tebbutt and her husband, David Tebbutt, arrived at a Kenyan island resort in September 2011, she sensed something was wrong. "It was completely quiet. When I was told there was nobody there except us, that felt really strange," she recalled to the BBC. "The room we were in was so far away from the rest of the building. But David said, 'Don't worry, this will be our *Robinson Crusoe* experience.'"

Instead, their African safari vacation turned into a horror story. Awakened their first night in the resort by the sounds of her husband struggling, Judith felt a rifle barrel jab her and was pulled off the bed. "I just saw this look on David's face. He looked really frightened," she recalled in an interview with *The Guardian* in 2013. "I shouted, 'What's happening?' and he didn't look in my direction."

She was dragged out to the beach. Barefoot and clad only in her pajamas, Judith was tossed into a speedboat and taken to Somalia, located about 25 miles away.

For the next six months, the British woman was held in a small, dirty room by a gang of Somali pirates. She was fed only potatoes and rice and subjected to regular humiliations and threats of execution. A mental health worker by profession, Judith kept herself sane—and alive— by extracting control over her situation, and her captors, anytime she could. She learned a few

Tebbutt barely ate during her imprisonment and says that by the time she was released, "I just looked like a skeleton with skin draped over her."

Hotel worker Ali Babitu Kololo (in the green shirt) was found guilty of robbery with violence in 2013.

words in Somali so that her captors would see her as a person, not merely a means for ransom. "I challenged them all through my captivity," she said. She exercised and did Pilates to keep her body in shape. Eventually, when she was allowed to speak on the phone with her son, Ollie—who told her that her husband had been killed—she confronted the man she believed to be the leader. "I said, 'It was you. You killed my husband!' and it was like this face-off," she remembered. "I thought, I'm just going to look at you until you turn your face away. I just felt such hatred."

Working through a private security company, not the British government, an unknown amount of money exchanged hands, and Judith was released in March 2012.

"I am, of course, hugely relieved to at last be free, and overjoyed to be reunited with my son, Ollie," she said in a statement. "This, however, is a time when my joy at being safe again is overwhelmed by my immense grief, shared by Ollie and the wider family, following David's passing."

In 2013, a resort employee was found guilty of robbery with violence for guiding the kidnappers to the Tebbutts' villa. Originally sentenced to death, his term was reduced to life in prison, the only person to face charges in the kidnapping. ⚓

"I felt that they saw me as this thing that they were going to make money from. They had no real interest in me as a person, or as a woman. Not at all."

JUDITH TEBBUTT

Restless Phantoms at Pirates' House

Ghosts prowl this Georgia tavern that used to be a sailor hot spot

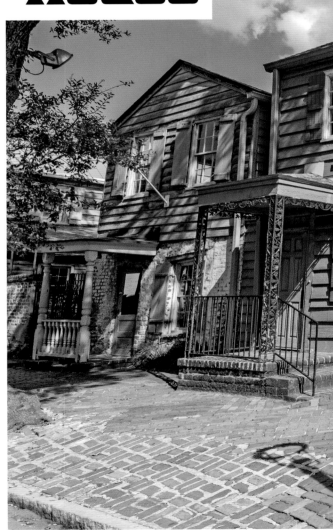

A drinking hole favored by ruffians, rogues and all other forms of salty, seedy characters from the waning years of the Golden Age of Piracy, this Savannah, Georgia, tavern built in 1734 holds the title of the oldest bar in America—and one of the most haunted.

In Pirates' House's rum cellar, where men were kidnapped and forced to serve at sea, visitors insist they've heard a voice growl, "Get me brandy. Get it, I say!" The gruff demand is attributed to the ghost of one Captain Flint. As he only existed in the pages of *Treasure Island*, these sightings may have more to do with the powers of alcohol than paranormal activity.

Still, in Savannah, where legends blend easily with reality, the Pirates' House and its famous network of secret underground tunnels built during the Civil War stir the imagination. Some believe these tunnels were critical links in the Underground Railroad, which slaves followed to freedom. They may have also been used to quarantine the city's yellow fever victims.

Aboveground, spooky figures are said to glide through the Pirates' House's rooms and stomp on the floorboards. Some insist they have seen—and photographed—images peering out from windows when nobody was there. ⚓

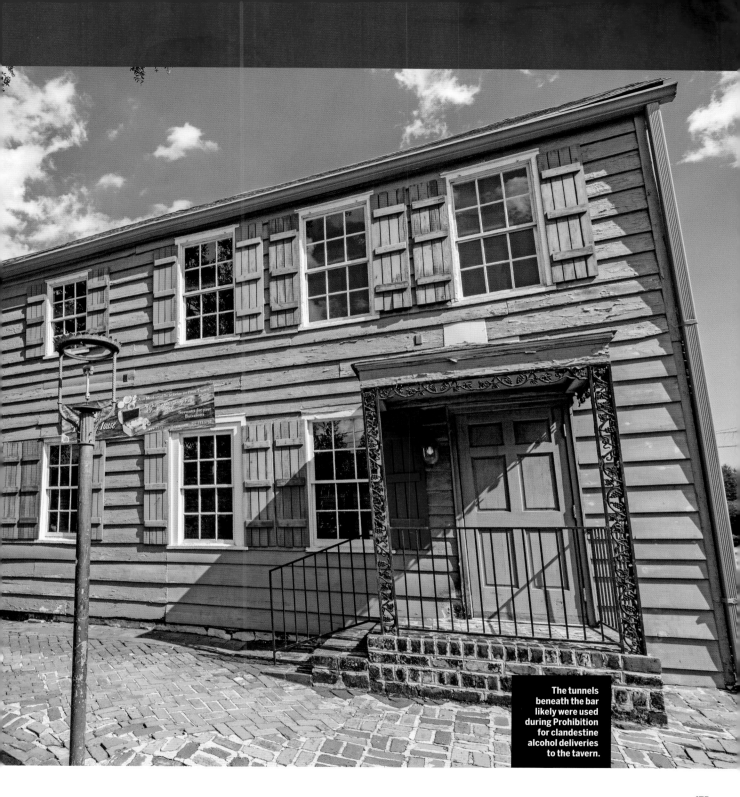

The tunnels beneath the bar likely were used during Prohibition for clandestine alcohol deliveries to the tavern.

"The legend of Jean Lafitte survives in the history and mystery of south Louisiana, where Lafitte's bayous and backwaters still meander toward the Gulf of Mexico."

NATIONAL PARK SERVICE

After the War of 1812, Lafitte received a pardon from President James Madison—and returned to piracy.

A Buccaneer Lingers in New Orleans' Pirate's Alley

Jean Lafitte often returns to the scene of a fateful wartime meeting

The apparition haunting a quiet passageway lined with irregular, jagged cobblestones in New Orleans is often identified as Jean Lafitte. Legend has it the famous French pirate huddled here with General Andrew Jackson during the War of 1812 to negotiate the release of Lafitte's jailed brother, Pierre.

In exchange, Jean Lafitte would lend his considerable maritime skills to the United States military in its latest war against Great Britain. That Lafitte emerged as an unlikely hero for Jackson's forces against British warships in the Battle of New Orleans lends some credence to the story, though no historical record backs up the clandestine meeting in what would come to be called Pirate's Alley.

William Faulkner may put some stock in the tale: He moved to a second-floor room at 624 Pirate's Alley to fuel his writer's imagination with the lurking apparitions.

Some say the Lafitte story is only half right: There is a ghost, but it's not his. According to another legend, a young pirate named Reginald Hicks fell desperately in love with a French Creole woman named Marie Angel Beauchamp. Wanting to marry her so that their child would not be illegitimate, Hicks could find only one priest willing to officiate: a German minister being held in the Old Parish Prison that runs alongside Pirate's Alley.

Hicks married his bride at the prison gate but was soon killed in the War of 1812. Searching for the child he could never meet, Hicks is said to return to Pirate's Alley, where visitors report hearing wedding bells and laughter when the alley is empty. ⚓

OLD ABSINTHE HOUSE, NEW ORLEANS
QUARTERS OF THE PIRATE
LAFITTE IN 1807

Lafitte's headquarters

"In a way, I do regret it, and in a way, I don't, because it's given me a lot of lessons, it's given me a lot of opportunities that I wouldn't have had…. Everything happens to us for a reason."

AMANDA TEAGUE

The Woman Who Wed a Marauder's Ghost

Spoiler alert: Her marriage to 300-year-old Jack Teague didn't end in happily ever after

For Amanda Teague, love really is dead. The Irish woman says that in 2016 she married the ghost of 18th-century pirate Jack Teague after he introduced himself to her by interrupting her meditation. They got to talking, found they had a lot in common despite the three-century age difference, and legally wed on a ship in a ceremony officiated by a shaman, with a medium speaking for the long-deceased Jack.

After she went public with her marriage, Amanda brushed off the inevitable media mocking. "If you believe in God or angels, if you believe in anything that's not of this earthly realm, then you believe in spirit," she told *The Washington Post* in July 2019. "So why would you find what happened to me beyond the realm of possibility?"

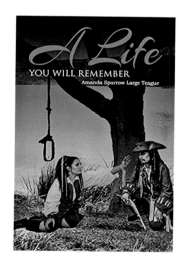

That's not the only pirate with whom Amanda connected. In 2015, she became an impersonator of *Pirates of the Caribbean*'s Jack Sparrow, even writing a book (pictured below) on her spiritual relationship with the character.

Sadly, people change, and so do ghosts, and Jack started getting too needy. "He was basically like an energy vampire," she said, explaining that she suffered health problems that she attributed to her husband. "When spirits stay around too long, they need an energy source and unfortunately Jack was using me as an energy source." So in December 2018 they divorced via an exorcism. "I would really say to people who are thinking about getting into this: Be really, really, really careful," Teague advised. "And if somebody is not telling you about the dangerous side of it, run a mile." ⚓

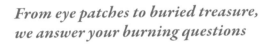

Fact or Fiction?

Pirates often wore their loot— including jewelry—for safekeeping.

From eye patches to buried treasure, we answer your burning questions

Pirates were not a literate lot, so little of how they actually lived is recorded in their own words. Much of what we think we know about pirates actually comes from fiction writers and Hollywood. So what's true and what's not about these seafaring outlaws?

DID THEY WEAR EYE PATCHES?

Pirates did lose eyes in accidents and battles, and they did cover them with patches. Historians believe the first pirate to wear a patch was Persian Gulf buccaneer Rahmah ibn Jabir al-Jalahimah, who had lost an eye in a battle in the late 1700s, long after the Golden Age of Piracy ended. But that's not the only reason pirates wore the iconic black patches. One theory holds that before raiding a ship, pirates would cover one eye. When they went below deck, where there was little natural light, they'd remove the eye patch and then be able to see well enough to fend off opposing sailors or search out booty.

Most of the rum consumed during the Golden Age of Piracy was made in the Caribbean.

Prosthetic hook

Peg legs weren't common

DID THEY WEAR EARRINGS?

With no secure place to store their personal belongings, pirates tended to keep everything they owned on their person. This included their jewelry—and they did wear a lot of it: gold chains, pendants, rings and anything else they had stolen. This bling set them apart from merchant and navy seamen, who were forbidden to wear jewelry, and served as a not-too-subtle warning to other ships of what they were about to lose. It also acted as something of a life insurance policy. When a pirate died, the jewelry would be sold to pay for a funeral. They did prefer hoop earrings and small studs, though not because it made a fashion statement: They believed that an earring pressing against their earlobe helped ward off seasickness.

DID THEY HAVE HOOKS AND PEG LEGS?

Life aboard a pirate ship was a dangerous business, and accidents and battle wounds often cost crewmen limbs. In this era before antibiotics, the best way to stem infection was amputation, which was performed by a ship's surgeon—or, if the vessel didn't have one, the carpenter or cook. There was no anesthesia and success rates were, unsurprisingly, low. Once the pirate healed, he could be fitted with a prosthetic hook or a wooden leg. An English pirate named William Condent was known as Billy One-Hand and a famous 16th-century English privateer named Christopher Newport lost his right arm while attacking a Spanish ship. Credit *Treasure Island*'s Long John Silver with his peg leg and *Peter Pan*'s Captain Hook for the association of prosthetics with pirates.

DID THEY DRINK RUM?

As the song says, "Yo ho ho and a bottle of rum"— pirates did like their alcohol (see page 30). They drank to celebrate their success and to forget their hardships. "Such a Day, Rum all out, Our Company somewhat sober," Blackbeard wrote in his journal. "A damn'd Confusion amongst us!" The men on Mary Read and Anne Bonny's ship

"The rum issue is no longer compatible with the high standards of efficiency required now."

THE BRITISH ADMIRALTY BOARD, WHICH IN 1970 ENDED THE PRACTICE OF ISSUING SAILORS A DAILY RUM RATION

Washington Irving, James Fenimore Cooper and Edgar Allan Poe wrote stories featuring pirate maps, but they were rare in real life.

Treasure wasn't usually buried

(see page 110) got so drunk after capturing a prize that the two women were the only ones left to fight when their ship was raided. As water went bad on ships, pirates primarily drank beer or wine, which lasted longer. They also drank gin and a concoction called bumbo, which was rum, lemon juice, grenadine and cinnamon or nutmeg, or flip—made with brandy, ale, lemon juice, sugar, egg yolk, cloves and cinnamon. Rum would also be downed in shots or mixed with spices to make grog. Surprisingly, sailors in the British Navy were given daily rum rations for centuries until the practice ended in July 1970.

DID THEY MAKE TREASURE MAPS?

There are no accounts in the historical record of any pirate marking an "X" on a map to show where his cache was buried. In fact, there are no known treasure maps. This was a trope that was invented by Robert Louis Stevenson in *Treasure Island*. The only real pirate who buried his treasure was Captain Kidd, and that was done hastily when he was on the run. Plunder normally was stashed on board the ship and didn't last long once the ship got into port. Pirates expected to have short life spans, so they tended to spend their shares of loot as quickly as possible in the brothels and taverns.

A scurvy cure

DID THEY KILL ALL OF THEIR PRISONERS?

The criminals of the sea didn't want to wage major battles to take over ships. It was dangerous and could be costly, to both the crew and the ship. Among their intimidation tactics were frightening visuals like hoisting the Jolly Roger flag (see page 52) or in the case of Blackbeard, smoke-filled hair (see page 74) to scare their victims into submission. So pirates didn't kill many people aboard the ships they captured—largely because if it became known that pirates took no prisoners, people would fight to the death, making victory more difficult. There is no record of the most famous pirate of all, Blackbeard, ever killing anyone. They weren't all as compassionate: On the flip side were bloodthirsty men like François l'Olonnais (see page 92) and the merciless Englishman Edward Low. Described by Sir Arthur Conan Doyle as "savage and desperate," Low tortured, mutilated and burned his captives, even forcing prisoners to eat the heart of their captain.

DID THEY DIE FROM NOT EATING ENOUGH FRUIT?

Scurvy—caused by a lack of vitamin C—was a common affliction aboard ships, with one British expedition to the Pacific Ocean losing 1,300 of its 2,000 men to the condition, which caused bleeding and swollen gums, weakness and fatigue, rashes and red spots. It is estimated to have killed more than 2 million sailors between the late 1400s and the mid-19th century. Explorer Captain Cook recommended eating sauerkraut, while others suggested placing a piece of turf on a patient's mouth to counter the "bad qualities of the sea air." In 1747, British surgeon's mate James Lind, who was traveling on the HMS *Salisbury*, conducted one of history's first clinical medical trials, treating 12 men suffering from scurvy with daily remedies that included a quart of cider or half a pint of sea water, two oranges and one lemon, "elixor of vitriol" (sulphuric acid and alcohol), or two spoonfuls of vinegar three times a day. A week later, those who ate the citrus fruit were well enough to help nurse the others. But it took four decades for those in charge of the Royal Navy to order the distribution of lemon juice to sailors.

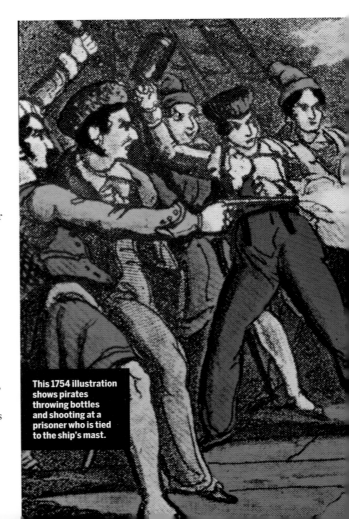

This 1754 illustration shows pirates throwing bottles and shooting at a prisoner who is tied to the ship's mast.

WHAT DOES "SHIVER MY TIMBERS" EVEN MEAN?

This old phrase, meant to express shock and surprise, refers to the splintering, or shivering, of a ship's wooden frame, known as timbers. It appears in print as early as 1795 in a serial publication called *The Tomahawk! or Censor General*, in which an old sailor says, "Lather me! Shiver my timbers," although in pop pirate culture the phrase became "shiver me timbers." Either way, the phrase was popularized in Stevenson's *Treasure Island* in 1883. Pirate Long John Silver uses the phrase or some variation like "shiver my shoulder" and "shake up your timbers" multiple times in the book. But

"The mariners were either crammed into their quarters like sardines in a box or slept, occasionally in good weather, sprawled like hounds on the deck."

HISTORIAN STEPHEN R. BOWN

most people know this phrase, like much of what is considered pirate talk, from British actor Robert Newton (see page 150). In the 1950 movie *Treasure Island*, he says in his West Country dialect, "Here's Jim Hawkins, shiver my timbers." ⚓

Test Your Cutthroat Knowledge

How much do you really know about pirates?

Blackbeard

1. WHAT WAS THE AVERAGE CAREER EXPECTANCY OF A PIRATE?
A One year
B Three years
C 10 years

2. WHICH PIRATE WAS KILLED AND EATEN BY CANNIBALS?
A Grace O'Malley
B François l'Olonnais
C Henry Every

3. WHICH PIRATE WAS THE FIRST CAPTAIN TO TAKE HIS SHIP AROUND THE WORLD?
A Francis Drake
B Blackstone
C William Kidd

4. WHICH PIRATE DID PETER PAN'S CAPTAIN HOOK SAIL UNDER?
A Blackbeard
B Henry Morgan
C Jean Lafitte

5. WHAT IS BLACKBEARD'S REAL NAME?
A Edward Teach
B Harold Winterbottom
C Bartholomew Every

6. WHAT IS THE TERM FOR THE SKULL AND BONES FLAG PIRATES FLEW?
A The Red Dagger
B The Bleeding Heart
C The Jolly Roger

7. WHAT WAS BARTHOLOMEW ROBERTS' PIRATE NAME?
A Red Roger
B Yellow Tiger
C Black Bart

8. WHAT DID PIRATES CALL A SHIP THEY SEIZED AND PLUNDERED?
A Booty boat
B Prize
C Goldship

A well-dressed pirate captain

Barbarossa

9. WHAT WERE BUCCANEERS NAMED AFTER?
A Buckteeth
B Wooden bucket
C Barbecue rack

10. WHICH 1950S MOVIE STAR POPULARIZED THE PIRATE SPEECH WITH ROLLED R'S?
A Robert Newton
B Tyrone Power
C Zane Grey

11. WHAT IS THE NAME FOR A SAILOR LICENSED BY A GOVERNMENT TO RAID ENEMY SHIPS?
A Corsair
B Buccaneer
C Privateer

12. WHAT MODERN-DAY COUNTRY IS ON THE ISLAND OF HISPANIOLA?
A Cuba
B Florida
C Haiti

13. WHAT DOES BARBAROSSA MEAN IN ENGLISH?
A Barbarian
B Barber
C Red Beard

14. WHICH CAPTAIN DID ANNE BONNY AND MARY READ SAIL WITH?
A Calico Jack
B François l'Olonnais
C Long John Silver

15. WHY DID THE LIONESS OF BRITTANY ATTACK ONLY FRENCH SHIPS?
A To defend England
B To avenge her husband's death
C To find greater treasure

16. JOHNNY DEPP DREW INSPIRATION FOR HIS JACK SPARROW CHARACTER FROM WHICH MUSICIAN?
A Kurt Cobain
B Keith Richards
C Dee Snider

17. THE OUTLAWS OF THE SEA USUALLY BURIED THEIR MOST VALUABLE TREASURE.
True
False

18. PIRATES OFTEN MADE VICTIMS WALK THE PLANK.
True
False

19. MUSICIANS PLAYED AS SHIPS WENT INTO BATTLE.
True
False

20. PIRATE CREWS DEMOCRATICALLY ELECTED THEIR CAPTAINS.
True
False

1: B, 2: B, 3: A, 4: A, 5: A, 6: C, 7: C, 8: B, 9: C, 10: A, 11: C, 12: C, 13: C, 14: A, 15: B, 16: B, 17: False, 18: False, 19: True, 20: True

CENTENNIAL BOOKS

An Imprint of
Centennial Media, LLC
40 Worth St., 10th Floor
New York, NY 10013, U.S.A.

ISBN 978-1-951274-62-7

Distributed by
Simon & Schuster, Inc.
1230 Avenue of the Americas
New York, NY 10020, U.S.A.

For information about custom editions, special sales and premium and corporate purchases, please contact Centennial Media at contact@centennialmedia.com.

Manufactured in Singapore

10 9 8 7 6 5 4 3 2 1

Publishers & Co-Founders Ben Harris, Sebastian Raatz
Editorial Director Annabel Vered
Creative Director Jessica Power
Executive Editor Janet Giovanelli
Deputy Editors Ron Kelly, Alyssa Shaffer
Design Director Martin Elfers
Senior Art Director Pino Impastato
Art Directors Olga Jakim, Natali Suasnavas, Joseph Ulatowski
Copy/Production Patty Carroll, Angela Taormina
Assistant Art Director Jaclyn Loney
Photo Editor Jenny Veiga
Production Manager Paul Rodina
Production Assistant Alyssa Swiderski
Editorial Assistant Tiana Schippa
Sales & Marketing Jeremy Nurnberg